T H E
MORNING

His empty tomb means more than you ever dreamed

Kim Allan Johnson

Pacific Press® Publishing Association
Nampa, Idaho
Oshawa, Ontario, Canada
www.pacificpress.com

Edited by Tim Lale
Designed by Tim Larson
Cover photo by Photonica®

Additional copies of this book may be purchased at
http://www.adventistbookcenter.com

Library of Congress Cataloging-in-Publication Data

Johnson, Kim Allan, 1947-
    The morning : His empty tomb means more than you ever dreamed/Kim Allan Johnson.
        p. cm.
    ISBN: 0-8163-1875-1
    1. Jesus Christ—Forty days. 2. Seventh-day Adventists—Doctrines. I. Title.

BT485 .J64 2002
232.9'7—dc21

2001058077

02 03 04 05 06 · 5 4 3 2

Dedication

This book is affectionately dedicated to my wife, Ann, and my daughter, Stefanie, for their unconditional love and unflagging support.

Acknowledgments

I want to publicly thank the following people who were a vital part of making this book a reality:

My wife, Ann, and daughter, Stefanie, who are my very best friends and most dedicated reviewers.

Jan Ellis, Gloria DePalma, Larry Yeagley, Diane Thurber, Sandra Doran, and Dale Slongwhite, who read rough drafts and provided valuable advice and encouragement.

Randy Maxwell, who has been an ongoing source of inspiration.

Dr. Ivan Blazen, who graciously gave expert counsel on theological issues.

As the author of *The Morning,* I would enjoy hearing from you. Share your reactions and comments by contacting me at the following email address: kallanjohnson@compuserve.com

Foreword

My father, the author of this book, is not only a thoughtful and gifted writer of biblical history, but he is also a careful and sentimental preserver of our family's history. Our basement floor and shelves are laden with precious artifacts that encapsulate, for future generations, the most significant Johnson moments. The widely varied collection includes my fourth-grade science project made entirely of pom-pom balls, several deflated basketballs, and a large, nondescript rock unearthed in our family's ancestral home—Cape Breton Island, Canada. All of these things my dad has managed to save from my mother's annual desire to purge the cellar of what she unthinkingly perceives as mere debris.

Amidst the piles, there are a few truly priceless items, such as a scrap of paper complete with hastily penciled tick marks in my dad's hand that represent the frequency of my mom's contractions just before she gave birth to me. About a month ago, my dad, lovingly reviewing his collection, unearthed another such treasure. It was an audiotape made when I was only about five years old. When my dad found it, he excitedly called my mom and me into the living room and popped the tape into a tape recorder with a look of gleeful expectancy on his face. At first, all we heard was the low hum of audio static. Then my dad's voice, in the spirit of Dan Rather, broke in, announcing himself as a roving reporter who had procured a time machine and was about to interview the apostle Paul, formerly known as Saul, played by an enthusiastic preschool me.

As the tape rolled on, I answered my dad's creative and amusing questions in a British accent, which was not only completely unconvincing, but also terribly out of place for a first-century disciple from the Middle East. Neither of us won any Oscars for our performances, but the laughter, creativity, and excitement that clearly permeated the recording reminded me why making such tapes with my dad was always one of my favorite Sabbath activities. Even as a young kid, these skits made the ancient and distant world of the Bible come alive. I felt, in these mock interviews, that the Scriptures were fresh and relevant for me in the present moment.

These tapes represent only one of the many ways in which my dad, throughout my life, has made religion and spirituality vital realities for day-to-day living. Now that I am an adult, his books have this effect of activating and empowering the Bible's truths. Our faith is rooted in stories that can have great historical interest, or vast future significance, but too often pass us by entirely as we struggle with the challenges of the present. The Resurrection is one such story. This book, *The Morning,* takes Christ's historical resurrection, along with the assurance of a future second coming, and powerfully fuses them by reminding us of their infinite significance for the present. Pick up this book and find yourself standing at the mouth of the empty tomb, encouraged and renewed by its promise for you today. Of course, I am certainly a biased critic, so I encourage you to read on and discover the hope and joy in *The Morning* for yourself.

Stefanie Johnson,
Daughter of the author

Contents

Introduction

Christ the Lord is risen today,

Alleluia!

Sons of men and angels say,

Alleluia!

Raise your joys and triumphs high,

Alleluia!

Sing, ye heavens, and earth reply,

Alleluia![1]

I am a plant killer. I don't mean to be, but I am. When I bring a new plant into my office, I can almost hear the poor thing say, "Oh, no, not Kim's room. Please, anywhere but here." As people walk by it pleads, "Hey, you, take me outta here." I don't care what kind of plant it is, I'll inadvertently, but most assuredly, do it in.

Just down the hall is another office I call the Plant Rehabilitation Center. Whatever green thing you bring in there, it thrives. It's like magic. Suppose the person manning the Center and I have identical plants, with the very same soil, sunlight, and watering schedule. After one month mine will have the flu, and the other one will be happily shooting out lush leaves and stunning blossoms. Mine will be coughing and wheezing, and the other one will be throwing parties. What makes the difference? I don't have a clue. Out of compassion, though, I've switched to silk.

The most amazing horticultural feat I know is growing something directly from seed. The person begins with a little, shriveled-up, rock-hard seed and nurses it into a sprawling cucumber vine or towering sunflower. From my vantage point, as a gardening moron, that is a never-ending source of wonder.

There is probably nothing on earth that looks so unpromising as seeds. They appear so lifeless and dead, so devoid of any possible future. If it weren't for the picture on the front of the package, who would ever guess that they could be good for anything but bird food? I can even imagine the seed itself harboring serious doubts as it eyes the plump, juicy red tomato on the label. "I can't be in the right package. No way. There's some colossal mistake here. Look at me. Is this somebody's idea of a joke?"

Utilizing a gardening metaphor, Christ said, " 'The kingdom of heaven is like a grain of mustard seed which a man took and sowed in his field; it is the smallest of all seeds, but when it has grown it is the greatest of shrubs and becomes a tree, so that the birds of the air come and make nests in its branches' " (Matthew 13:31, 32). He predicted His ministry would, at some point, look lifeless and then experience amazing growth.

I don't know of any time when Jesus' kingdom looked more like a shriveled-up mustard seed than during the period between His death and resurrection. That had to be the absolute low point. The disciples were reduced to a quivering group of demoralized men. It is amazing to think that today's sprawling, worldwide tree of Christianity, with its millions of converts, tens of thousands of churches, mega-million dollar budgets, magnificent choirs, and intrepid missionaries was once a tiny seed of fainthearted hideaways. The disciples thought the Jesus movement was over and hid in the upper room waiting for the Passover to end so they could sneak back to Galilee before the authorities crucified them too.

"Everything that they had believed in and had hoped for was swept away by a mighty darkness. All that was left was a vast and barren desert, and in this desert they were stranded.

"They gave up all hope. They could hardly move. They thought to themselves: 'What is the use of going on? Everything is meaningless.' "[2]

The one thing that dramatically and permanently changed all that was Jesus' resurrection. It galvanized His followers and was the soil out of which the early church was born. No resurrection, no Christianity. The apostle Paul put it this way, "If Christ has not been raised, then our preaching is in vain and your faith is in vain" (1 Corinthians 15:14).

The apostles would be appalled today at how seldom we make a big deal over the Lord's resurrection in our church services and programs. The early church dwelt on that theme over and over like a drumbeat. Luke tells us, "And with great power the apostles gave their testimony to the resurrection of the Lord Jesus, and great grace was upon them all" (Acts 4:33).

George Ladd observes, "The first recorded Christian sermon was a proclamation of the fact and significance of the resurrection.... Peter said almost nothing about the life and earthly career of Jesus.... The all-important thing was the fact that Jesus who had been executed as a criminal had been raised from the dead." (See Acts 2:14-36.)[3]

When the Christian church was in its infancy, the primary function of the apostles was to confirm the truth of Jesus' resurrection through their eyewitness testimony.[4] When the disciples were attempting to find a replacement for Judas, they insisted that the person had to have personally seen the risen Christ. (See Acts 1:22.)

The Lord's resurrection was integrated into the life of the New Testament church in many ways. It was one of the two truths that people needed to accept in order to be saved. "If you confess with your lips that Jesus is Lord and believe in your heart that God raised him from the dead, you will be saved" (Romans 10:9). It was also one of the six basic truths taught to new converts. (See Hebrews 6:1-3.)

Coupled with the Cross, the truth of the Resurrection sent shock waves throughout the ancient world and won countless hearts, from priests to paupers. Without question, " 'the resurrection of Christ is the very citadel of the Christian faith. This is the doctrine that turned the world upside down in the first century.' "[5]

Some time ago I witnessed a thought-provoking scene on television that involved a seagull. Having grown up on Cape Cod, I have little sympathy for seagulls in general. I will never forgive the one that deliberately soiled my dark suit in a mean-spirited fly-by just as I was about to board a ferry to preach on a nearby island.

All that prejudice aside, there is one seagull that stands out, whose image lingers. I was eating breakfast in front of our TV, watching the countdown for the launch of the very first space shuttle. The huge rocket stood poised on its massive pad, leaking vapor, shedding thin sheets of frost, anxious to thunder into outer space. The commentator talked about the incredible power that would soon come roaring out of the engines in a deafening inferno. In moments the very ground would quake. All spectators had to be miles away to avoid injury. The TV cameras were equipped with special long-range lenses that gave the viewer the best seat in the house.

"Ten, nine, eight . . ." I leaned forward, my muscles tensed. "Seven, six, five . . ." Suddenly, from the right edge of the screen a seagull came into view flying less than one hundred yards in front of the space shuttle. It flapped along as it had done countless times, oblivious, contented, enjoying the view, scanning for food. "Four, three, two . . ." The seagull undoubtedly saw the spacecraft but had no idea of the implications for its life. "One." If the seagull somehow survived, can you imagine the conversation at the birdy dinner table that evening!

In A.D. 31, the Roman soldiers at Jesus' tomb were conducting business as usual. Then something happened, so immense, so unexpected, so shattering, that at first they could only babble about it incoherently. Earthlings in general had been going about their daily routines for centuries, caught up in relatively minor matters, when " . . . three, two, one," Christ emerged from the tomb in glory, and the world has never been the same.

The Scriptures record that Christ rose "early in the morning" (Mark 13:2, KJV). Morning represents renewal, fresh beginnings, and hope. The resurrection of Christ captured all those meanings and invested them with infinite depth. The sun and clouds could never partner to create as wonderful a dawn as the morning Jesus banished death forever and made the darkness flee. He dramatically fulfilled the psalmist's prediction, "Weeping may endure for a night, but joy cometh in the morning" (Psalm 30:5, KJV).

It is at Calvary and the empty tomb that we lay the foundation of the Christian life. Those momentous events enable us to see the truth about God's love and understand the key issues in the wrenching battle between Christ and Satan. We see a Savior who is Victor over all that is evil and destructive. We find forgiveness for our sins and the assurance of salvation. We discover the basis for a life of hope and witness a power that can turn our brokenness and shame into spiritual wholeness. Without taking time to adequately build every stone in that foundation, our spiritual experience can easily be reduced to a burdensome religion of guilt and fear.

Lifeless, matter-of-fact presentations of vital spiritual topics can never move human hearts the way God intended. In an attempt, therefore, to capture both the factual and emotional content of the stories surrounding Jesus' resurrection, I have at times employed my imagination to portray various scenes. These fictional portrayals seek to be faithful to the inspired record and are documented whenever possible.

The Spirit could do such fantastic things in and through the first disciples because Christ was so wonderfully real to them. They had walked intimately with the Son of God for years. Peter wrote, "We were eyewitnesses of his majesty" (2 Peter 1:16). They sobbed at what they saw on Calvary and erupted with immense joy at the appearance of their risen Lord. As we journey together through the Resurrection story, it is my prayer that, like the disciples, you too will come face to face with that same Jesus of great tenderness, power, and unquenchable love.

---

[1] *Seventh-day Adventist Hymnal* (Hagerstown, Md.: Review and Herald, 1986), #166.

[2] Morton Kelsey, *The Drama of the Resurrection* (Hyde Park, N.Y.: New City Press, 1999), p. 10.

[3] George Eldon Ladd, *A Theology of the New Testament* (Grand Rapids, Mich.: Eerdmans, 1974), p. 317.

[4] Ibid.

[5] *Seventh-day Adventists Believe ... A Biblical Exposition of 27 Fundamental Doctrines* (Washington D.C.: Ministerial Association, General Conference of Seventh-day Adventists, 1988), p. 115.

Chapter 1

Love's Last Breath

Once the criminals were nailed and the crosses stabilized, events on Golgotha settled into an eerie time of waiting. The most noticeable activity during much of that period was Jesus' battle to breathe. Watching a crucified man struggle for air could be an unnerving spectacle even for the most callous observer. The scene was similar to an exhausted, drowning swimmer repeatedly thrashing up from the sea.

Breathing on a cross took enormous effort and concentration. Every new breath was a trade-off between several more seconds of life and searing jolts of pain. The victim had to press down on nail-pierced feet in order to take the pressure off the diaphragm and draw in a few more precious liters of air. By way of analogy, imagine each breath you take being preceded by a dentist drilling into your unanesthetized nerves.

Christ's mouth gaped open, with foamy, blood-tinged spittle running down one side of His bearded chin. The Savior's bare chest heaved in and out several times a minute as He desperately clung to life until all was finished. The shuddering, raspy sound of each hard-won inhalation could be clearly heard amidst the general socializing on the hill. It was not unlike the labored wheeze of an asthma attack. His helpless followers hung on every priceless breath, hoping desperately for a miracle.

Jesus' mother carefully monitored His erratic breathing. Her eyes were riveted on Christ's torn lips and flaring nostrils. Mary's mind drifted back over the years to when her Son emerged from her womb and drew in His first infant breath. She remembered when, as a youngster, He loved to blow out the candles at the end of joyful Sabbaths and memorable feast days. She recalled the time He emerged from the cool waters of Galilee gasping for air during His first boyhood swimming lesson.

Standing weak-kneed on Calvary, holding her hands over her mouth in sorrow, she now wondered how many more breaths her Son could possibly have left. One? Thirty? A hundred? Mary knew His breathing intimately. She had listened so many nights with a mother's fine-tuned ear as Baby Jesus inhaled and exhaled right next to her bed. She had listened then with a mother's innate concern for congestion, wheezing, or worse, silence. It was that same dreaded silence that she listened for so intently now, on that terrible, suffocating crucifixion day.

I never knew what it was like to have one's hopes and dreams hang on a loved one's every breath until the long, dreary night I watched my mother die. Dad and I kept vigil over Mom's unconscious, cancer-riddled form as she slowly slipped away. It was as if she were drifting out to sea while we stood helpless on the rocky shore, yelling through cupped hands, "We can't bear to be separated from you. We love you so much. Never forget that we love you."

After months of tests, treatments, nausea, and pain, my beloved mom came home to live out her final days. On that seemingly eternal last night, a single lamp cast a soft, familiar glow around her favorite corner room. Curled up atop an adjustable hospital bed, her withered frame formed only a slight rise under the freshly laundered sheets. On the wall above her head hung pictures of us kids and of better days gone by. Two sounds defined the night, her shallow, uneasy breathing and the periodic whir of the morphine pump dispensing blessed relief directly into her IV-laden arm. Dad spoke resignedly of an expected "death rattle." He had seen death up close before, both within his own family and as a fireman. He appeared utterly downcast and drained.

During the night, the interval between Mom's breaths grew steadily longer. Anticipation clutched at our throats as we involuntarily coaxed her exhausted lungs to keep going. Each new breath meant she was still with us, that our family was still whole. Each inhalation cheated death for a few more moments. But by morning, she was taking only occasional wisps of air, surely not enough to sustain life.

Then, at 6:50 A.M., my precious mother breathed no more. I turned to Dad and said, "I think this may be it." He bent over and put his face right next to hers, listening very carefully. Seconds seemed like hours. At last he turned toward me and tearfully said, "She's gone."

I have never been so consumed with breathing and not breathing before or since. I got on very intimate terms with a subject I would have much preferred to know nothing about at all.

On Passover Friday, Mary was also consumed with just such heartrending matters. Her hopes rose and fell with each of her Son's costly gasps. As she kept watch on Golgotha, her leftover grief from the death of Joseph once again crept out of its hiding place, doubling her sense of loss. She could feel her head start to pound and feared she might faint. She turned to John, leaned heavily on his arm, and laid her weary head on his thickly muscled shoulder.

Finally, about 3:00 P.M., Christ's hot, depleted lungs drew in a large gulp of air, and He startled everyone by shouting, "It is finished. Father, into Your hands I commit My spirit." Then, the One who had breathed pure life into Adam before the onslaught of sin, hung His head and died. It was the last, tortured breath of love.

*   *   *

Imagine someone named Dave entering his local hospital to visit Frank, a terminally ill friend. Dave exits the elevator on the fifth floor, shuffles down the highly polished, tiled corridor, and follows the signs marked "Cardiac Intensive Care." After pushing open the large double doors to the ward, he is startled to hear people cheering. Upon entering his friend's cubicle, Dave sees family members and close acquaintances exchanging high-fives and hugging each other joyfully. The atmosphere is reminiscent of the day three years before when the local basketball team won the state championship.

Stunned, Dave finally manages to ask someone what this is all about. The person smiles and answers, "Frank just died. Isn't it wonderful? It just doesn't get any better than this!" Immediately Dave thinks, *These people are nuts.*

*   *   *

That startling, incongruous, fictional scene is similar to what actually happened in heaven the moment Jesus died. When Christ's life ended, *"there was joy in heaven. Glorious* to the eyes of heavenly beings was the promise of the future."[1] Beings throughout the universe had undoubtedly been glued to the Cosmic News Network, watching with rapt attention every second of our Lord's cruel trials and subsequent journey up Golgotha's hill. They agonized with Him as the nails were hammered home. They cringed at the callous mockery and verbal abuse. Millions of angels and unfallen beings collectively gasped in horror when Christ screamed out, "My God, My God, why have You forsaken Me?" Many turned away, sickened with grief.

17

But, as soon as Jesus actually died, the scene in galaxy after galaxy changed dramatically. Suddenly everyone's heart was filled with undiluted happiness and joy. Even though they probably didn't give high-fives, they surely found otherworldly ways to express their jubilation.

How could they have such an upbeat reaction? How could they rejoice at Jesus' death? A few possibilities come to mind. They knew that Christ had gained an incredible victory for all eternity and was now beyond the reach of Satan. They also understood that from the Trinity's point of view, raising the dead is no big deal. The Creator can very easily re-create. The Savior's resurrection was only a matter of time. "He'll be alive again soon for sure," the unfallen universe exulted. "No grave can hold Him now." From their point of view, delirious celebration was the order of the day.

If we turn our gaze back to earth, however, we see a far different reaction to Jesus' death among His followers. All morning and afternoon they had watched Christ's life drain away on the cross. When He actually bowed His head and died, every lingering dream of future glory was demolished. They could see only darkness and despair ahead. Looking up at His lifeless form, they were not thinking about a resurrection for several reasons.

First, He looked so utterly defeated. The Romans and the Jews had clearly won. They succeeded in debasing Him beyond belief. We can hardly imagine the mental and emotional distance the disciples traveled between Palm Sunday and Passover Friday. Sunday was the inaugural parade down Pennsylvania Avenue, the ticker-tape celebration along Fifth Avenue in New York. Tens of thousands hailed Christ as a conquering hero. Then on Friday, He became a pariah. Crucifixion was reserved for the most despicable criminals. Today we might think of rapists, child molesters, traitors, drug lords, or mass murderers. In A.D. 31, on just such a list of humanity's sewage, there appeared the lovely name of Jesus.

Second, resurrection seemed unthinkable because Christ looked so irreversibly dead. Some people die so peacefully and with such a well-preserved physical form that you might easily think they had simply drifted off for a good night's sleep. They hardly seem dead at all. Someone could almost say, "Let's tip-toe out of the room now and let them rest."

But not so with Jesus. There was no question that life had completely drained out of Him, every ounce of it. He looked like an animal that a ravenous lion had bitten by the neck and shaken hard, over and over, until the victim's torn, lifeless form hung limply from the beast's vicelike jaws. Terrible wounds covered Christ from head to toe. Long, deep, lacerations crisscrossed His skin. Countless swollen, oozing welts and bruises blanketed His frame. He hung painted in His own blood. Adding death to death, a soldier expertly placed the tip of his razor-sharp spear between Jesus' left middle ribs and callously shoved it deep into His heart, destroying vital tissue and creating a copious flow of fluids.

Third, resurrection appeared ludicrous because this time the Resurrector Himself had died. It was one thing for Jesus to resurrect others even when, like Lazarus, they had been dead four days and started to rot. But what happens to faith when the Life-Giver Himself so brutally passes away? What happens to hope when the Miracle-Worker Himself has been beaten and pounded into a crumpled heap of skin and bones? What happens when the teeming waters are dried up at their source? No one had ever brought himself out of the grave before. We might just as easily imagine a cardiac surgeon repairing his own diseased heart. Ridiculous!

More than the Savior died that Passover afternoon. The horror of what Jesus' followers saw destroyed their belief. Like the sound of multiple electrical switches clicking into the "off" position, you could almost hear faith shutting down in countless hearts. As if caught in a huge blackout, hope flickered and then went out, plunging the entire region into deep spiritual and moral darkness.

You could stare into people's eyes and see it all so clearly—grief, disillusionment, anger and despair. "With the death of Christ the hopes of His disciples perished."[2] The faith of hundreds of followers, from the inner circle to the fringes, shriveled up and died. Even the faith of Mary His mother, Mary Magdalene, and the beloved John withered in the face of such overwhelming loss.

Jesus' unexpected death presented His followers with a very sticky problem—what to do with the body? The Romans loved to let corpses decompose and putrefy on Calvary, while birds of prey and wild animals ate them at their leisure, leaving behind only the skull and various sun-bleached, indigestible bones. Nothing deterred criminal activity better than such a horrific, in-your-face display of shredded body parts, accented by the stench of decay.

Refined Jewish sensibilities, on the other hand, rejected such barbarous methods and demanded that bodies be taken down before sunset. Not that the Pharisees cared a fig about the dead person. They simply didn't want the carefully cultivated religious atmosphere of the city to be compromised. After all, who wants to see a dead body lying among the roses at Disneyland or a corpse bobbing down a broiling river at Yellowstone National Park? It's clearly bad for business. Therefore the Sanhedrin generously provided an infamous mass grave outside Jerusalem for just such garbaged human beings.

The apostle John hated the thought of an ignominious burial but was powerless to prevent it. The earthquake and lightning had scared most people off the hill, and the apostle stood nearly alone beneath the silent middle cross. The soldiers had already dislodged one of the thieves and dumped his body to one side. They were working on the second thief, tugging and cursing at the nails. Jesus would soon be next.

Where on earth are James, Peter, Andrew, Thomas, and the rest? John thought.

Staring up at Jesus' motionless form, he whispered verses from the Psalms to calm his racing heart. Flies gathered on Jesus' body, picking at the wounds, crawling in and out of His mouth and nostrils, buzzing about His tear-encrusted eyes.

Suddenly Joseph of Arimathea came puffing up the road carrying a bucket of water, tools wrapped in a dark blue cloth, and a piece of paper bearing Pilate's scribbled signature. (See John 19:38.) Approaching the centurion he commented, "Here. I've got special permission from the governor for that man's body. I'll take care of it myself. I've made all the arrangements for burial in my own tomb over there." He pointed toward the northwest.

Recognizing the respected rabbi, the puzzled centurion waved him along, saying, "He's your responsibility now."

Joseph had riches, power, a lofty position, and a reputation for unfailing fairness and honesty. I imagine he had been a promising religion student from his earliest days in Arimathea, graduating summa cum laude. He eventually moved to Jerusalem and was taken under the wing of Israel's most venerated rabbis. His entire family rejoiced as they watched him climb up through the ecclesiastical ranks until he finally reached the pinnacle of national pride by being appointed to the exclusive, almighty Sanhedrin.

Over the years his influence grew, until everyone in the streets of Jerusalem recognized him immediately. He might be compared to a United States senator today, one who occupies a large ornate office, has several loyal staff members, and moves easily in the circles of the elite.

But as soon as Joseph made the fateful decision to request Christ's cadaver, he put his career, reputation, and bank account on the line. He identified himself with a man condemned for blasphemy by the Jews and fingered as a traitor by Rome. He was willing to trade the work of a lifetime for a future of rejection, ridicule, and scorn. And for what? There was nothing to be gained.

The same could easily be said about Nicodemus. Both men were willing to give up everything they had for a despised dead man.

Joseph's new tomb was, without question, extremely expensive.[3] He knew that after the burial of Christ, the tomb could never be used again because Jewish law strictly forbade it from being utilized after a criminal had been placed there.[4]

"We'll wait for my friend Nicodemus," Joseph instructed. "He's gone for spices and linen. It's only an hour and a half 'til sunset, but we'll do what we can."

Soon the unlikely trio of daring undertakers was struggling to pry out the nails. As each nail was removed part of the heavy, filthy body slumped downward. "Grab His legs," Joseph uttered. Nicodemus could feel the Savior's knotted calf muscles and the crusty edges of scabbed-over wounds. Tears flowed freely as they eased Christ onto the ground and stood over Him silently for a few moments, staring at His twisted, battered form.

"How much suffering He endured since the Passover meal," John observed.

The young disciple knelt down, took a sponge from the bucket of water, squeezed out the excess, and began washing away the blood as much as possible.[5] Pink rivulets ran off the Savior's torso, forming little pools on the hard, uneven ground. Cleaning up the body was harder than they anticipated, especially around the shoulders, back, and buttocks, where deep wounds had repeatedly been scraped by the rough-hewn wood of the cross. The matted hair and numerous puncture wounds ringing the scalp were caked with blood. The task was at once revolting and yet strangely comforting, to be able to touch his Master once again. The sickening smell of sun-baked blood, dried sweat, and putrid spittle would be etched into John's memory forever.

They laid the Savior onto a clean linen sheet. Nicodemus walked a few yards away and retrieved a large, dark-brown bag. He tipped it up, held the end open slightly then shook some of the sweet-smelling, powdery mixture of myrrh and aloes over Jesus' body. He would eventually use 75 pounds in all. Only the very wealthy could afford such extravagance.

Each man grabbed a corner of the linen, and they trudged off together as best they could, toward the tomb a hundred and fifty yards away, across an old rock quarry. Their feet searched for sure footing amidst the jagged chunks of stone left from ancient digs.[6]

"Just a little farther," Joseph encouraged. "Over there."

The newly created tomb lay in a surprisingly beautiful garden, ringed by fruit trees, with angled rows of hyssop and lilies forming a garland of color. (Mary Magdalene would later name the gardener as a suspect in the disappearance of Christ's body.) The three struggled to get Jesus' dead-weight body up a final incline and through the opening of the tomb. Joseph entered first, tugging on the linen. The other two followed.

The yellow-orange rays of the waning sun shone through the doorway, illuminating the dust particles the men stirred up. John had never been inside such a large, elaborate tomb before. A stale, dank, musty odor assaulted his senses.

They wrapped Jesus' body in linen strips from the shoulders down. The rest of Nicodemus's gummy aromatic spices were placed between the layers. They served as a preservative, helped offset the stench of decay, and hardened like cement to glue the cloth into a solid cocoon. The body was then lifted onto a waist-high shelf and gently pushed into place.[7]

John leaned against the rough rock wall next to the shelf, let his head drop to his chest, and coughed out racking, pent-up sobs. After a couple of minutes, Nicodemus stepped over and placed his hand on John's heaving shoulder. "There's nothing more we can do now, son," he offered. "It's time to go."

Before leaving, John glanced back one last time then stepped out into the crisp evening air. He drew in a deep breath, exhaled heavily, and suggested they say a brief prayer. "Oh God," he began, "we are broken in spirit. How could all this have happened? Please watch over this place and over our dear Friend." He paused and with breaking voice added, "And give us strength to hold on to You." They put their shoulders against the round entrance stone, braced their feet on some protruding rocks, and with great effort rolled it slowly into place.

Several days after my mom's funeral, I stood over her grave staring down at the newly placed marble gravestone. It read in part, "Dorothy Hunt Johnson. Date of Death: November 23, 1992." As I read and re-read those words, the reality of her death seeped into the very marrow of my bones. My mind became fixated on the six feet of earth that now lay between us. I worried about her spending the upcoming winter out there alone in harsh weather. I wanted to run, yet also wanted to linger near the one who had sung to me in my crib, baked my favorite blueberry pies, and inquired so earnestly about my days. I bent down, picked up some stray brown leaves and twigs that had blown onto her grave, crushed them in my fist, and flung them aside. Tearfully I mouthed the words, "Goodbye, Mom," and turned to leave.

John, Joseph, and Nicodemus must have felt a similar, yet far deeper sense of loss. John found himself staring numbly at the outer rock wall of the tomb. Initial shock now ebbed into a sharper, more piercing inner pain. His head throbbed. He wiped his tear-filled eyes with the back of his sleeve. Finally, the three disciples exchanged brief words of sympathy, looked over at the downcast women observing about thirty feet away, and parted for home amidst the elongated shadows of impending night.

---

[1] Ellen G. White, *The Desire of Ages* (Nampa, Idaho: Pacific Press Publishing Association), p. 769, emphasis supplied.

[2] Ibid., 772.

[3] Leon Morris, *The Gospel According to Matthew* (Grand Rapids, Mich.: Eerdmans, 1995), p. 727.

[4] Ibid.

[5] Ellen G. White, *The Spirit of Prophecy,* vol. 3, "At the Sepulcher."

[6] Raymond E. Brown, *The Death of the Messiah* (New York: Doubleday, 1994), 2:1279.

[7] *The Seventh-day Adventist Bible Commentary* (Hagerstown, Md.: Review and Herald, 1956), 5:551.

Chapter 2

Peter's Grief

Note: This chapter and the next explore the grief of two of Jesus' most devoted followers: Peter and Mary Magdalene. No one loved the Savior more than they, and no one suffered more deeply at His death. We will enter their dark despair so that in subsequent chapters we can see the Resurrection through their ecstatic, flabbergasted eyes. By entering their pain, we can later enter more fully into their overwhelming joy.

Modern Christians have never known the heartbreak of the believers in A.D. 31 who witnessed Jesus' death. We have never buried our heads in our hands thinking that Christ had been utterly defeated by the powers of darkness. We have never felt the anguish of believing that the incredible movement Christ so carefully built up was now in ashes. That life-sapping perspective, that despairing point of view was, however, very real to Jesus' closest companions two thousand years ago.

Self-recrimination and guilt clutched at Peter's throat. How could he have committed such an awful deed? How could he have failed so miserably? If only he could relive the last few hours and change what he had done! Cold air reddened his face as he raced headlong into the moonlit night. The quietness of the city at this early hour exaggerated the sound of his sandals pounding along the hard soil of Jerusalem's crooked streets. A dog bared its teeth and barked angrily. In the distance a donkey brayed. A shadow slipped into an alleyway between two small homes. Tears poured down the disciple's cheeks as he stumbled on.

He ran past closed shops, empty wagons, shuttered windows, low stone walls, tethered horses, through one of the city gates and finally out through the thick city wall. He stopped, glanced around at the endless rows of pilgrim tents dotting the hills across the Kidron Valley, then continued his mad dash down a rock-lined road. His breathing became increasingly labored, and his heart hammered within his chest with more than the physical strain of his desperate odyssey. Eventually, he scrambled through the iron gate to Gethsemane, halted after several more steps, shrieked out in self-loathing, and shivered in shame.[1]

There is no question that Peter terribly wronged His Lord. At Christ's trial before the Sanhedrin, when the Savior most needed loyalty and support, the apostle repeatedly denied any connection with Him. But if the headline in the local newspaper read, "Peter Denies Lord!" the editors would have completely missed the heart of the story.

We usually focus exclusively on the fact that Peter sided with the enemy. Yet, if we looked more deeply into the disciple's heart, we would see something noble there as well. What compelled Peter to enter that Jewish den of lions to witness Jesus' trial? What drove him to risk his life hanging around the hate-filled home of Caiaphas? None of the other disciples except John dared to go near the place.

More than anything else it was Peter's all-consuming love for his Master that drew him like a magnet to the dangerous judgment hall that fearful night. Christ meant everything to him, and he had to be with his Lord.

All during Jesus' ministry, Peter's ventures invariably turned sour because of his woeful self-reliance and spiritual immaturity, but they were all rooted in his tremendous devotion to the Savior. Impassioned love for the Son of God was the motivation behind all his major blunders. Repeatedly during Christ's ministry, it was Peter's burning affection for Christ that got him in way over his head, sometimes quite literally.

For instance, there was the night the disciples encountered a furious storm on fickle Galilee. (See Matthew 14:22-33.) Jesus had earlier ordered the Twelve to leave in a boat for Capernaum, across the northern end of the Sea of Galilee, normally a journey of only about an hour. After dark, however, a fierce storm burst upon the lake. Putting up the sail was unthinkable. After eight tortuous hours of rowing, they found themselves still at sea, floundering at the mercy of the waves.[2] Christ had quieted another ferocious storm just six months before. (See Matthew 8:23-27.) Now the disciples were again in desperate straits, but this time without their Lord. The boat lurched back and forth like an enraged animal. Several passengers threw up. The disciples' fingers gripped the oars and seats like a vice.[3] At any moment they could be swallowed up in death.

Suddenly, a flash of lightning illuminated a figure moving across the tumultuous sea, striding on the tall, white-capped billows. The disciples' mouths dropped open. Grown men screamed out in terror. Finally someone recognized the mysterious form and yelled, "It's the Lord!"

Overcome with joy, Peter had only one thought: *I've got to be with Jesus!* He cupped his big hands over his even bigger mouth and yelled into the wailing winds, "Lord, if it's really You, ask me to come."

That had to be the craziest idea ever! No one in human history has ever wanted to be with Christ so badly that he attempted such an impossible task. Other than Jesus, Peter had never seen a fellow human being walk on water, especially atop such a killer sea. If it were me, I would have tried walking on the water *inside* the boat first. But after the Lord yelled back, "Come," the apostle sat on the heaving rail, placed one leg over the side, and then the other. He leaned forward, pushed away, and stood on angry waters up to one hundred and thirty feet deep.[4]

We often scold Peter for showing off as he tiptoed across the waves. We usually highlight how embarrassingly he failed. But look what he failed at! Peter was the Wilbur and Orville Wright of water walking.

After he launched out, a wave hid Christ from view.[5] Apparently, Peter was in a trough and couldn't see over the top. Imagine how big that wave had to be in order to block his view of Christ. Five feet? Six feet? Huge. And he's out there walking on it!

To put the apostle's deed in perspective, picture a man staggering down the center aisle of your church during a worship service, mumbling to himself, "I'm such a dummy. I'm such a nincompoop."

You approach him and see a long, bloody gash across his forehead. You ask, "What happened?"

He replies, "Oh, I was just flying around, didn't watch where I was going, and bumped into the top of that tall pine tree across the street."

"Sir," you respond in amazement, "you were flying without any plane or hot air balloon or anything?"

"Yeah," he says, "but I'm such a failure."

"Sir," you interrupt, "no one has ever done that before in the history of the human race!"

And that's what Peter did that dramatic night on the broiling lake. It wasn't primarily pride or a desire to impress his associates that initially made him step out of that reeling boat. Love put him out there. He longed to be with his Lord.[6]

The apostle's spiritual weakness got him in trouble along the way, but Jesus must have smiled when Peter yelled back, "Ask me to come." The real failures that night were the disciples who played it safe and sat glued to their wooden seats. They didn't sink, but they didn't experience the exhilaration of water-walking faith either.

On another occasion Peter's love for the Master got him in trouble way over his head in the Garden of Gethsemane only a few hours before the denials. (See Matthew 26:47-56.)

The disciples had slept through one of the most important events in history—Jesus' thrice-repeated prayer for deliverance. Then around midnight they awoke to a terrible emergency.

During my growing-up years, my dad belonged to a volunteer fire department. His bedroom was crammed with enough radio receivers to operate a small army. Whenever there was a fire somewhere in town, his radios blared out an insistent alert signal—*Aaaarp! Aaaarp!*

The huge horn mounted atop the firehouse also screamed into the night—*Wah-Baw! Wah-Baw!*—imploring volunteers to come.

My father, who could get into his fire-fighting duds faster than Superman in a phone booth, would yell upstairs, "Kim! Hey, Kim! Let's go! Hurry up!" I remember well the initial disorientation of waking with a start in the middle of the night, enveloped by all those urgent sounds.

The disciples also awoke to disorienting sounds—the shouts and cries of an angry posse hustling into Gethsemane around midnight to arrest Jesus. The crowd consisted of Roman soldiers, temple police, priests, elders, scribes, Judas, and the rabble of Jerusalem.[7] Scores of lanterns and torches illuminated furious eyes, bearded faces, long robes, spears, sticks, and various farm implements people had picked up to crush any resistance. The flames cast everything in a yellowish-orange tint.

Jesus courageously stepped out in front of the disciples and demanded that the mob let them go. Two soldiers marched forward, grabbed Christ's hands, callously wrenched His arms behind His back, and started to bind them with rope.[8] Standing about ten feet away, Peter reacted instinctively. In an attempt to defend his Savior, the large fisherman pulled back his robe, unsheathed his sword, and raised it high over his head. Having grown up in a rough seacoast neighborhood, he was no stranger to the usefulness of a weapon. Yelling, "Let Him go, you idiots!" he rushed forward and attacked Malchus, the nearest villain. (See John 18:10.)

Moonlight glinted off the blade of the sword as it slashed downward. At the last moment, the victim caught a glimpse of Peter's arm and tilted his head to the right. Instead of slicing the man's skull open like a melon, the enraged apostle only managed to cut off his left ear. The detached ear fell onto the man's shoulder, then flopped to the ground. The wounded servant let out a desperate scream and clutched the side of his head. Blood spurted through his fingers, ran down his arm, and stained the upper portion of his blue-striped robe. Jesus quickly released Himself from the soldier's grip. He then held Peter back with one hand

and reached out to touch the gaping wound with the other. Instantly a grade A, custom-designed, wax-free ear appeared, the same size as the other.

In a few seconds, Peter would tell the disciples to run for it, but in this remarkable act of defense, he exhibited astonishing bravery. The Bible says that the crowd consisted of a "great multitude" including a "cohort" of professional Roman soldiers from the Fortress of Antonia. (See Matthew 26:47; John 18:3.) A cohort was a military term for up to six hundred men in arms.[9] With rumors of a potential riot running rampant, at least one or two hundred soldiers would not be unlikely. And here was a former fisherman taking them all on single-handedly! The use of force was a huge mistake, but Peter's primary motivation was, once again, deep love for the Savior.

And now we come to the most dangerous, heart-rending situation Peter's love for the Master ever got him into. Shortly after the arrest, he and John entered the home of Caiaphas, the high priest in the heart of Jerusalem. (See Matthew 26:58-75.)

To picture the high priest's home, imagine a two-story palatial house built around a tennis court. This inner courtyard contained fountains, flowerbeds, shaped shrubs, marble-lined walkways, and lush hanging plants. It smelled of predawn dampness, boiling meat, smoky torches, and woolen wraps. It was in this enclosed courtyard that Peter denied having anything to do with Jesus.

Charcoal embers glowed from an iron basin, giving off a little heat and a muted, reddish glow. Peter sat apprehensively among the crowd around the fire, shuffling his feet and blowing on his hands. He hoped that people would think he was a member of the mob that had arrested Jesus and therefore would avoid detection as one of His disciples.[10]

The young maiden who greeted at the door studied him carefully and concluded, " 'You also were with Jesus the Galilean' " (Matthew 26:69).

The anxious apostle turned on the young woman as if she were an attacking wolf and tried to keep her at bay with the angry words, " 'I don't know what you are talking about' " (Matthew 26:70, NLT)! Somewhere nearby, a cock crowed.

Though identified as an accomplice, Peter refused to run away. He attempted to avoid further attention by joining in the rough crowd's ridicule of Christ.[11] He jested, "That Nazarene must have gotten into some old barracks wine or something to be talking like he does."

Shortly after that, he looked over at the lighted judgment hall, witnessed the abuse of Christ, and inadvertently let his true feelings spew out. "Haven't those insane rulers ever heard of something called justice! They're the ones who should be on trial tonight!"[12]

Hearing his irate outburst, another maid pointed an accusing finger and declared too loudly, " 'This man was with Jesus of Nazareth' " (Matthew 26:71). Peter denied it, this time with an oath.

Luke then shares the remarkable detail that after the second denial Peter still hung around the courtyard for a full hour. (See Luke 22:59.) In that hostile situation, an hour could seem like an eternity. Peter was in a much more precarious position than John because he could be arrested at any moment not only for being a follower of Christ, but also for the much more serious charge of attempted murder back in Gethsemane. Though twice fingered by Jesus' enemies, the apostle was nonetheless loath to leave.

To see Peter's denials as only cowardly attempts to save his own neck is unfair. Surely self-preservation was part of his thinking. But if all he cared about was his own safety, he would never have stayed in the courtyard as long as he did. The end does not justify the means, but Peter's denials were rooted to a large degree in his tenacious desire to remain near his Lord.

A close relative of the man Peter tried to murder eyed the apostle next. "Didn't I see you in the Garden? We know you are one of his disciples, for we can tell by your Galilean accent." (See Matthew 26:73.)

Peter had a distinctive northern accent. His version of Aramaic didn't employ the deep guttural, throaty sounds used by the Jews of Judea. Imagine an undercover northern soldier during the Civil War letting a few hard "r's" slip while trying to mingle with Confederate troops in Atlanta. Or picture a soldier from the South trying to blend into a crowd in Boston and saying, "Don't ya'll just hate them Southerners?" Likewise, Peter's dialect got him into very hot water at Jesus' trial.

In another ploy to hide his true identity, he made the third denial while swearing a blue streak. (Jesus' disciples had a reputation for not swearing.) Peter could undoubtedly recall plenty of foul language from the old days at the nets, and he included it when he shouted, " 'I don't know the man' " (Matthew 26:74, NLT)!

While the denial was fresh on his lips, the cock suddenly crowed a second time. The shrill sound came from somewhere over the wall to Peter's right. The high-pitched clarion rang out in sharp, unmistakable tones above the noisy crowd. It pierced the crisp night air and lingered overhead as if frozen in time. Peter heard it from beginning to end, every bit of it, more clearly than he had ever heard anything before. He spun around in the direction of the crowing, and his mind instantly recalled the impossible prediction, "You will deny Me." A sense of panic and alarm swept over him. His knees weakened.

When Christ heard this last, vehement denial, He turned toward His wayward follower. At the very same time Peter felt drawn to look directly at his suffering Master.[13] Their eyes met and were locked onto each other for several extraordinary, unforgettable moments. It seemed to Peter that the two of them were suddenly alone. The rest of the world was completely blotted out. All that mattered was the penetrating gaze of His Lord. Jesus' tear-filled eyes glistened in the torchlight. In the Savior's lingering look, the apostle saw only extraordinary love, understanding, and forgiveness, and it changed him forever.

The disciple also focused on another image that would haunt his mind for years. The whole time Jesus looked at His sinful follower, the Savior's lips were quivering.[14] Peter's callous words hurt the Savior so deeply that it made His lips quiver in godly sorrow. The chief disciple's repeated disavowals tore at Jesus' heart. Christ's lips also quivered because He drew all of Peter's searing pain into Himself. Though suffering terrible abuse, the Savior thought only of Simon's desperate need. Jesus' timely, compassionate look kept Peter from falling further and making a complete shipwreck of his faith.

A soldier's callous blow snapped Jesus' head sharply to the left.[15] Peter could stand it no longer and rushed heartbroken from the dreadful scene. Being recognized three times by his enemies didn't drive Peter from the judgment hall. It was the grief-stricken look of his Lord that sent him racing out into the night. He stumbled through the darkness and eventually wound up in Gethsemane.[16] Drowning in self-hatred, he leaned against a gnarled olive tree, wept bitter, gut-wrenching tears, and wished that he could die.

There were two of Jesus' followers who wanted to die that terrible night, Peter and Judas. Judas couldn't believe that God loved him enough to forgive him, and he went out and committed suicide. The tree he chose on which to hang himself was right next to the Via Dolorosa, the road leading from Jerusalem to Calvary.[17] Judas knew that Christ would have to pass that way carrying a cross, and the betrayer chose that spot on which to die as a final, despairing farewell.

Peter suffered through an agonizingly dark period after the denials. He beat himself up mentally knowing that he had dealt the most hurtful blow of all to Christ. But unlike Judas, he never completely gave up on God. He hung onto a glimmer of hope. In the midst of utter despair, Peter stepped back from the edge of spiritual ruin when he remembered how intensely Jesus had always loved him.

As he stood there in the Garden, Peter recalled how Jesus had consistently believed in him. From the beginning, Christ focused not primarily on his glaring faults but on what he could become by grace.

For example, when the Lord first met Peter, He changed his name. (See John 1:41, 42.) Think how odd that name change must have felt. Suppose you visited a church and the first thing the greeter said was, "Your name is Robert, but from now on it will be Fred." Or, "Your name is Sally, but from now on it will be Susan."

Wouldn't you be thinking, "This person belongs in an institution"?

But that's exactly what Jesus did when He initially saw Peter. He said, "Your name is Simon, but from now on it will be Peter." That new name means "rock." It is not Mt. Everest like Jesus, but nonetheless a substantial stone. In that name alteration Christ assured Peter that He saw a day when the apostle would be like a solid spiritual rock. No more self-dependence. No more rash decisions. No more wavering or pride.

I have some insight into the importance of a name because of the semi-uniqueness of my own. Ninety-nine percent of the people in America named Kim must be women because I regularly get free samples of cheap perfume, incredible deals on *Ladies Home Journal,* and piles of junk mail addressed to "Miss" Kim Johnson. Several years ago I pressed Mom on the issue, and she confessed she had expected a little girl. Names can shape our attitude toward ourselves and the attitude of others toward us as well. Who knows what my life might have been like if I'd been tagged Butch or Bruno?

Jesus grasped Peter's large, callused hand, looked him straight in the eye, grinned, and said, "Hi there, Mr. Rock Man." That name became a personal prophecy, full of hope and encouragement to persevere.

Hope also awakened in the Garden when the apostle remembered Jesus' words in the upper room. " 'Simon, Simon, Satan demanded to have you, that he might sift you like wheat, but I have prayed for you that your faith may not fail' " (Luke 22:31, 32). Peter now clung to that word *but* with all of his might.

He thought, *Jesus knew all about the denials and prayed for me anyway. He knew all about my disavowals and cared for me still.* Peter poured out his hurt in genuine repentance and dared to believe that Christ had already forgiven him long before the arrest, long before He ever reached the judgment hall.

Nonetheless, Peter didn't know how he could ever forgive himself.[18] Oh, how he wished he could apologize to Christ in person. How earnestly he would profess his loyalty once again. "I'm so sorry, Jesus! I didn't mean to hurt You. I was so terribly afraid."

The Savior had opened a whole new world to the fisherman from little Bethsaida Julias, and Peter loved Him for it.[19] Peter had the raw intelligence and natural leadership ability of a Franklin D. Roosevelt or Winston Churchill. But he moved in very small circles and lived in a small mental box—until Jesus found him. It would be like Einstein walking up to a man in rubber coveralls working the docks of Gloucester, Massachusetts, and saying, "Follow me. I'll show you things you've never imagined."

The headstrong disciple had invested his entire future in the itinerant Rabbi. He and the Savior endured so much together, laughing and weeping together as intimate friends. They walked countless dusty roads, talked often by open fires, and frequently slept under the stars. Christ awakened within him such compelling dreams, such buoyant hope. Peter had just begun to believe in himself, believe he could, in fact, become the leader Jesus wanted him to be. And now this! How deeply it all hurt! The stinging sense of loss and the denials that kept playing over and over in his head nearly crushed him.

In Gethsemane, the first light of Friday morning brushed the horizon with beautiful yellow and pink pastels. Dawn ignited the tips of the tallest trees and illuminated the Garden in soft, gentle light. Peter took out the sword still hidden under his cloak, stared at the bloodstained blade, and thought once again of turning it on himself. A minute later he flung it angrily far into the woods. The sound of metal pinging off a distant boulder broke sharply upon the early stillness.

Looking down through tears, Peter saw what appeared to be three or four spots of dark blood on the ground next to his right sandal.[20] Puzzled, he moved his foot aside and realized that he had been standing on a cluster of reddish dots. Instantly there flashed into his mind the image of Christ standing over him in the moonlight barely six hours before. He vividly recalled the streaks of fresh blood on the Savior's pale cheeks and the hoarse voice pleading, "Could you not pray with Me for just one hour?"

Horrified, Peter quickly stepped back. *Right here,* he thought, *right here Jesus prayed so desperately for me.* The grief-stricken disciple sank to his knees under drooping branches and buried his face in his hands. His body rocked back and forth, and his shoulders shook as he sobbed.

---

[1] Ellen G. White, *The Desire of Ages,* p. 713.

[2] *The Seventh-day Adventist Bible Commentary,* 5:415, 416.

[3] *The Desire of Ages,* p. 381.

[4] Siegfried Horn, *The Seventh-day Adventist Bible Dictionary* (Hagerstown, Md.: Review and Herald, 1960), p. 383.

[5] *The Desire of Ages,* p. 381.

[6] Ellen G. White, *Redemption: Or the Miracles of Christ, the Mighty One,* p. 62.

[7] *The Desire of Ages,* pp. 694, 695.

[8] Ibid., p. 696.

[9] Leon Morris, *The Gospel According to John* (Grand Rapids, Mich.: Eerdmans, 1971), p. 741.

[10] *The Desire of Ages,* p. 710.

[11] Ibid., p. 712.

[12] Ibid.

[13] Ibid., p. 713.

[14] Ibid.

[15] Ibid.

[16] Ibid.

[17] Ibid., p. 722.

[18] Ellen G. White, *Advent Review and Sabbath Herald,* 6 Feb. 1913.

[19] *The Seventh-day Adventist Bible Dictionary,* p. 868.

[20] *The Desire of Ages,* p. 713.

Chapter 3

Mary Magdalene's Loss

In the Gospel story no one loved Christ more extravagantly than Mary Magdalene. Her love for the Savior was rooted in her dramatic deliverance. It is an amazing story that is, surprisingly, seldom told.

Mary resided with her brother, Lazarus, and sister, Martha, in Bethany, about one and a half miles from Jerusalem, and just east of the Mount of Olives. At some point, a man from the same town, Simon the Pharisee, "deeply wronged" youthful Mary and led her into sin.[1] I doubt that he simply taught her how to pickpocket. Almost certainly the wrong he committed against her was sexual in nature.[2] And because Simon was Mary's uncle, he was, in fact, committing incest.[3]

Incest has been defined as " 'any sexual contact between an adult or older adolescent, perceived to be in a trusted family role with a child or adolescent.' "[4] Another author adds that incest "includes stepfathers as well as genetic fathers, uncles, brothers, and grandfathers."[5] So, as Mary's uncle, Simon qualifies.

The incest must have been kept a secret, because much later at the feast in Simon's home, one week before the Crucifixion, Jesus couched His reference to the Pharisee's sin in a parable to keep him from being publicly exposed and humiliated.[6] Nonetheless, the effect of that sexual abuse on Mary was utterly devastating.

I imagine Simon telling Mary to follow him into a corner room in his home. I can hear him speaking words to her that would be seared deeply into Mary's mind for the rest of her life. "I am a lonely man," he said, "very lonely. My days at the temple are long and tiring. I don't have anyone to give me the comfort and companionship that I need. I have been praying about it, and I believe God has specially chosen you to give me that intimacy and closeness."

He then approached Mary and tried to pull her to himself and kiss her. She pushed him away as hard as she could, stepped back in alarm and stood against the far wall, wide-eyed, with her hands over her mouth. Her heart pounded as she shivered in fear.

When she tried to refuse her uncle's advances, the hypocritical Pharisee offered an ominous reprimand. "I had hoped that you would be eager to please your elder. I am very disappointed in you. But I can tell you this, young lady, if you resist me or tell anyone, I'll make your name and that of Lazarus and Martha a shame throughout Judea. I'll have you all cast out of the temple. If you oppose me, you'll be shunned from here to Capernaum."

From that day forward, Mary suffered sexual abuse on a regular basis at the hands of her renowned relative. She felt trapped and utterly humiliated, caught in an unrelenting nightmare from which there was no escape. By sheer force of will, she kept up the visits in order to avoid the unthinkable consequences if she stayed away.

In Scripture, incest is cast in deep shame. For example, Amnon brought terrible disgrace on his sister, Tamar, by committing incest with her. Another brother, Absalom, was so outraged that he later had Amnon murdered. (See 2 Samuel 13:28, 29.) In Leviticus 20 the crime of incest is listed as punishable by the death penalty, either by stoning or fire.

Today we know more fully some of incest's awful effects. Susan Forward, a specialist in counseling incest sufferers, comments, "The victim is drawn into a world of secrecy—a world of shame, hopelessness, and guilt—where she feels isolated from everyone else. There is no one to turn to, no one to confide in, no one to ask for help…. She has feelings of betrayal and self-loathing."[7]

A researcher into the trauma of incest says that the victim "stands alone, holding the powerful secret, told that she will destroy herself and others if she reveals it. It is little wonder that with this confusion and despair, most incest victims contemplate suicide." [8]

Patty Barnes adds, "Incest is the most devastating and harmful form of child abuse that can emotionally cripple an individual for life."[9]

Night after night Mary cried herself to sleep. It appeared to her that the God she had loved so faithfully must have turned His back on her for some unknowable reason. She prayed over and over for forgiveness and a righteous heart, yet nothing changed. Eventually she could pray no more. The girl who once loved to sing felt every melody dry up within her. The young woman who had been so outgoing and optimistic about life now turned inward in shame. Waves of depression washed over her. She repeatedly pleaded with Simon to stop, but he turned a deaf ear and continued to use her as his own personal, unpaid whore.

At some point, Mary became utterly desperate. The only option she could think of was to run away. If she simply disappeared from the village forever, there was a good chance that Simon might not seek revenge. A week later, she secretly packed a few belongings and quietly snuck away.[10]

After leaving her beloved Bethany, Mary headed north toward to the town of Magdala. (The name Mary Magdalene means "Mary from Magdala.") She may have chosen Magdala because it was as far as she could get from home and still speak her native Aramaic. It was, without doubt, a journey of bewilderment and tears. Although about three days' journey geographically, it must have seemed like forever emotionally.

Initially, she might have tagged along in a caravan or with a group of pilgrims. They would take the usual route ten miles northeast to Jericho, then cross the Jordan River and head toward the purple mountains of Peraea to avoid Samaritan country. At Beth-haram the road veered north up the hot valley for forty or fifty miles. Somewhere beyond Mount Gilboa, she crossed back over the Jordan into the region of Decapolis, and finally made her way north again to verdant Galilee.[11]

During that fateful odyssey, Mary surely looked back in the direction of Bethany with a lump in her throat and periodically stopped to sit down in the nearby grass and cry. It was a journey that, for a single woman of the first century, would have been absolutely terrifying.

Magdala itself was a flourishing city on the fertile western shore of the thirteen-mile long, seven-mile wide, Sea of Galilee. Its name comes from the Hebrew word for "tower," *migdal,* which probably means that the town acted as some type of guard tower or fortress.[12] The entire region exported salted fish, bread, fruit, grains, figs, and olive oil throughout Judea. Situated on the turnpike from Mesopotamia to the Mediterranean and the main route to Nazareth, "Magdala—teemed with merchants, traders, and caravaneers. Roman legionaries…[and] Germanic mercenaries of the Herods."[13] Josephus put the population at around forty thousand.[14] Inhabitants spoke not only Aramaic but also Greek and sometimes Latin.

The nearby lake was "covered with ships and boats, engaged either in fishing or traffic, or carrying travellers or parties of pleasure from shore to shore."[15] The city had stores where pigeons were sold for sacrifice and shops for making fine woolen cloth, plus many other buisnesses.

Magdala had a reputation among the rabbis as a center of immorality, as did Tiberias with its thermal baths three miles to the south.[16] Its fall was later attributed to its licentiousness.[17]

Into this foreign environment walked the grieving Mary Magdalene. At some point, she entered the dark world of prostitution. We know she was a prostitute because of the way she is referred to later in Bethany, when she anointed Jesus' feet. One of the references to Mary in that story is variously translated as, "a woman who was living an immoral life,"[18] "the town harlot,"[19] "a woman of the streets—a prostitute"[20] (Luke 7:37). William Barclay also states, "The woman was . . . a prostitute."[21]

Whether Mary joined a brothel in Magdala or found customers on her own we do not know. Perhaps, as in Old Testament times, she sat at busy crossroads dressed to attract attention and waited for customers.[22] Many times harlots would frequent public places trying to lure men back to their homes.[23]

Mary undoubtedly drifted into prostitution out of dire financial necessity. Women of that day depended on their husbands for financial security.[24] The career options for single women were somewhere between slim and none. Mary may also have been drawn to prostitution as a result of the sexual abuse she suffered at the hands of Simon. "If [an incest victim] begins thinking she is nothing but damaged goods, a piece of junk, she can be victimized again . . . even prostituting [herself] in repeated sexual encounters."[25]

Prostitutes like Mary faced numerous dangers and indignities. Customers ran the gamut from those who were refined and well to do, to others who were demanding, abusive, unkempt, and reeked of body odor. She stuffed the client's payments into a moneybag that she hid away for safekeeping. She had no idea at the time that those same coins would one day purchase a rare perfume for her Savior.

The carefree days when Mary was a little girl must have seemed like such a distant dream. Her bleak inner world probably echoed that of some youthful, modern-day prostitutes.

Sheila, age seventeen: " 'Before long I began to wish that I'd never been born. I always felt ashamed and sickened by what I did.' "[26]

Marianne, age fourteen: "I always felt full of hopelessness.... A lot of young prostitutes are murdered every year. No one cares about these girls. They are somehow considered worthless; it's almost as if they weren't even human beings. These are the girls who live outside of respectable society."[27]

Lynn, age thirteen: "Whenever I'm with a trick I try to turn off my mind. I just block out the whole experience. Sometimes I imagine that I'm on a trip to India or on safari in Africa. Anything just so long as I don't have to deal with the fact that this is really happening to me. You've got to do that to survive. It helps some, but it doesn't always work. You can never really escape from your own horror."[28]

Emotionally numb from being treated for so long as a commodity, a rental property, Mary didn't dare allow herself to hope for anything better. Sadness was her most faithful companion.

And then came Jesus.

"A majority of the recorded incidents of Jesus' Galilean ministry took place in the vicinity of the Plain of Gennesaret, where Magdala was situated."[29] In fact, Jesus and His disciples sailed to Magdala after feeding the four thousand. (See Matthew 15:39; Mark 8:10.)

News reached Mary that a large crowd had gathered to hear a heralded itinerant teacher. He must have been a dynamic personage to draw people away from Magdala's famous Hippodrome, the large racing arena built for the predominantly Gentile population.[30] Out of curiosity, a deep sense of need, or a desire to solicit the crowd, Mary chose to see what the fuss was all about.

Around the Sea of Galilee, Christ usually taught outdoors, so she would typically have seen Him standing on a hillside instructing the multitudes. Tradition indicates that during that same time period Jesus gave His famous "Sermon on the Mount" in a little village named Tabgha, which was within walking distance of Magdala.[31] Mary could easily have attended and heard Him say, " 'You're blessed when you're at the end of your rope. With less of you there is more of God and his rule. You're blessed when you feel you've lost what is most dear to you. Only then can you be embraced by the One most dear to you' " (Matthew 5:3, 4, *The Message*).

The thick layers of hurt and cynicism that had formed around Mary's heart would not have allowed her to trust a man very easily, even this Man. As a twentieth-century prostitute explained, " 'I found it particularly hard to trust anyone. I couldn't shake the feeling that everybody in my life wanted to use me for one thing or another.' "[32]

Any faint feelings of hope within Mary would have been instantly squelched by the insistent inner voice of caution. Most likely, she spent several days listening to the young Preacher, watching from a distance as people from every type of background, with every kind of vice and disease imaginable, received Christ's acceptance and restoring touch. Light and darkness struggled within her.

Each day her fears lessened further, until at some point she felt herself moving forward with many others as if guided by invisible arms. Step by courageous step, she nervously made her way closer to the Rabbi, seeking healing from all her shame and regret, healing from her suffocating grief over lost family, lost joy, lost dignity, lost womanhood, lost self.

When she stood directly in front of the Savior, she simply hung her head and cried. Her shoulders sagged, unable any longer to bear the overwhelming load of hurt. Jesus' own eyes glistened with tears as He inquired, "Mary, do you want to be free from the demon that torments you so?"

"Yes," she whispered earnestly. Her entire body shook in anticipation.

He placed His hand on her head and prayed, "Heavenly Father, give this special young lady new life. Free her from the terrible grip of the evil one. Honor the longings of her heart today and make her whole."

Jesus paused, smiled, and said, "Go in peace." Mary took a few steps back then sank to her knees, emotionally exhausted and overcome. In the Old Testament, the penalty for harlotry was being burned or stoned to death, but Jesus' grace found a far better way.

The most amazing part of Mary's story is that she had to be delivered from the iron grip of her old way of life *seven separate times.*[33] The One who told Peter to forgive seventy times seven reached out repeatedly to this very troubled, desperate woman.

After Mary was healed the first time, she soon fell back into her old despondency and immoral life. Perhaps she was threatened by clients or became anxious about money or simply didn't value herself enough to sustain hope. She was delivered by Christ a second time and fell back. She was delivered a third time and fell back. It seemed impossible for her to remain faithful without Jesus at her side.

We don't know how many times she kept coming back to Christ on her own. With her background of abuse, it is likely that she gave up on herself long before the seventh healing. It is very possible that after the first few failures, she abandoned every glimmer of hope and let herself sink into even greater depths of depression, immorality, and despair.

And it would have been so characteristic of Jesus to seek her out as one of His precious lost sheep. I picture Christ knocking on her door. Knowing it is far too early for any of her customers, Mary inquires, "Who is it?" Silence, then another series of knocks. She steps toward the door, opens it and gasps. It's Jesus!

He tells her with great tenderness, "Mary, I heard the demon has returned. Some of My followers and I will visit you until you're fully well, until the last of your demons is destroyed."

Infinitely loving and persistent, Jesus refused to give up. Somehow, slowly, His faith and confidence resurrected her own, and she was delivered a fourth time. Soon, however, she fell back. Christ and His followers continued to listen to Mary's woes, wipe her tears, and offer her words of encouragement. Twice more Jesus knelt by her tormented frame and poured His heart out in prayer for her deliverance, and two more times she fell.[34]

But after the seventh healing, the demons returned no more. Finally she was free! Is it any wonder she loved the Savior so fiercely?

Beginning in the autumn of A.D. 29, Mary traveled with Christ during His second missionary journey through Galilee, gaining spiritual strength and maturity.[35] Jesus had to patiently and lovingly teach Mary to trust that she was indeed fully accepted and that He would never turn her away.

During the time Mary journeyed with Jesus, she would have personally witnessed Christ raising the widow of Nain's son from the dead; the healing of the blind and dumb demoniac and the demoniacs of Gadara; the stilling of the storm on Galilee; the healing of the woman with the issue of blood; and the raising of Jairus's daughter. She also would have heard Jesus' famous "Sermon by the Sea."[36]

Mary assisted those who came to Christ for healing and new life. She was part of a large group of women who cared for the Lord and His disciples by purchasing supplies with their savings, preparing meals, washing dirty robes, and mending worn sandals.[37] (See Luke 8:1-3.) Eventually she was able to make her way back home to Bethany.

About a year after returning home, Mary heard Jesus' awful prediction of His impending death and longed to honor Him in burial by anointing His body with the most expensive ointment she could afford. She reached into the corner of a bedroom drawer, pulled out all of her savings from years of prostitution, emptied the coins onto the bed, and counted. With a dark-blue woolen shawl thrown over her shoulders, she headed for the largest perfume and spice vendor in all Jerusalem.

After showing Mary a variety of perfumes, each costing more than the one before it, the store owner finally brought out a gorgeous, translucent, light-gray, alabaster container imported from Egypt.[38] He gently placed the jar down and looked at it with the pride of a parent viewing their newborn. "A container like this is for the rarest of perfumes," he said. "It can only be opened by breaking the bottle's long neck."[39]

He paused a moment then continued. "The ointment inside is pure nard with no contaminants whatsoever.[40] It is made from fragrant roots found high up in the distant Himalayan Mountains.[41] This is an ointment fit for royalty. King Herod himself would be pleased to possess it. I have never seen anything else like it in all my travels." (See John 12:3.)

Mary straightened and drew in a deep breath. After a long pause, she asked, "And how much are you asking?"

The owner snickered. "I'm sorry to laugh, but this is a treasure, you see. At today's values it is worth at least 300 denarii. I don't mean to embarrass you, but I did want you to know that we do carry the very finest." He began putting the perfume away. (See John 12:5.)

The value of 300 denarii was half again as much money as the disciples estimated it would take to feed ten thousand people. (See Mark 6:37.)[42] In the days of Christ, 300 denarii was equivalent to a full year's wages for a common laborer.[43]

Imagine how your family and friends would react today if you even thought about spending $30,000 for a small bottle of perfume! Wouldn't they be utterly shocked if you told them you might use your entire life savings to purchase a fragrance from Estée Lauder? And it came in a container that had to be broken open, forcing you to use all of it at once. No wonder the Gospel writers called it "exceeding precious" and "very costly." (See Matthew 26:7; John 12:3.)

That was the hefty price tag facing Mary Magdalene. Throwing reason to the wind, she opened her bag, fingered the coins, and replied to the shopkeeper, "I'll take it."

Mary must have been a prostitute for quite a while to accumulate such funds. It was forbidden for money earned from prostitution to be used to pay religious vows or for sacrificial purposes in the Jewish temple.[44] But in the hands of a devoted follower, those tainted funds were transformed into an exquisite offering to the Lamb of God.

The following Saturday evening Mary retrieved the perfume from its hiding place under her bed. She knew that Jesus would be attending a supper at Simon's home and saw it as the ideal opportunity to pour the costly ointment onto her cherished Lord. The disciples had informed her that Christ would not die, but would in fact soon be crowned King of Israel, and she wanted to be the first to show Him honor.[45] Her love for Christ overcame the natural revulsion of returning to the home of the Pharisee who had abused her so terribly years before. Thoughts of affection for the Savior filled her mind and dispersed the dark images of her earlier pain.

Clutching her beautiful container, Mary entered the portico into Simon's house and slowly approached the dinner table where Christ reclined. The ornate room buzzed with casual conversation. In the dim light she quietly stepped up behind the Savior.

Overcome with adoration, Mary dropped to her knees in worship. Her shoulders shook with emotion as years of pent-up feelings converged at that incredible moment.

An expert on the effects of sexual abuse observes, "Many women have stopped tears so long that they do not know how to cry. . . . Once women learn to weep, they seem to lose control over *when* they weep."[46]

Tears of gratitude flowed down Mary's cheeks and fell as an offering, one by one, onto Jesus' feet. Focused fully on Christ, she forgot it was shameful for a woman to let down her hair in public and used the long tresses to wipe the tears that moistened the Savior's skin. Grasping His feet, she kissed them repeatedly. (See Luke 7:37, 38, 45.)

At some point Mary broke open the lovely flask of perfume. Images of the deliverance in Magdala flashed through her mind. "Thank You, Lord," she prayerfully whispered as the liquid spilled onto Jesus' hair and ran down onto His thick neck. She glanced over at her brother, Lazarus, and recalled his stunning deliverance from the grave. Such amazing gifts Christ had provided! "Thank You, thank You," she repeated.

Mary spread the remaining ointment generously across His instep, down over His toes and heels. The sweet smell wafted throughout the room.

Judas's sensitive nose picked up the expensive aroma, and he immediately complained, "What a waste!" (Matthew 26:8, TLB).

When I attended college, it was the custom to buy a watch for your girlfriend when you became engaged. I remember scrimping and saving, shaking my piggy bank, scrounging through the debris in my dresser, picking through old pizza crusts under my bed, and inspecting every inch of my car to find enough money to purchase a decent watch at the local department store. Ann wore it proudly for the three months that it worked.

Now can you imagine one of my friends pointing at that shiny new watch on her wrist and saying, "What a waste"? That would have crushed my fiancée's heart. And Judas's observation that Mary had squandered the ointment on Jesus must have slammed into the Savior's soul as well.

Simon the Pharisee should have been sympathetic to Mary, having caused her downfall and having known personally, as a former leper, the shame of being an outcast. Instead, he self-righteously exclaimed, "What a wretched sinner!" His furrowed brow radiated loathing and contempt.

Poor Mary heard the criticism and trembled before her accusers. She recoiled as old, familiar feelings of guilt and rejection swept over her.

Jesus turned, reached out His hand, and lifted Mary's quivering chin. Looking with great compassion into her terror-stricken eyes, He smiled and came to her defense. " 'Why do you trouble the woman? For she has done a beautiful thing to me.... Truly, I say to you, wherever this gospel is preached in the whole world, what she has done will be told in memory of her' " (Matthew 26:10, 13).

What you don't understand, the Savior continued, is that " 'he who is forgiven little, loves little' " (Luke 7:47). Or, put another way, "he who is forgiven much loves very, very much." It may well be that during Jesus' upcoming sufferings He could still smell the aroma of that perfume on His skin, and it gave Him comfort and courage during His terrible ordeal.

All during the following week, Mary's heart trembled as the tension in Jerusalem escalated, with Jesus at the very center of the storm. Early in the morning of Passover Friday, she received the terrible news of Christ's arrest and raced to the Roman judgment hall. Standing amidst the maddened spectators, she heard Pilate's condemnation of Christ and screamed, "Let Him go! He's innocent!" over and over until she was hoarse.

She followed the horrible procession up from the city toward Calvary, fiercely pushing her way through the mob to catch a view of her battered Savior. She gasped when Jesus twice fell under the cross and anxiously strained to see if He would revive. As the soldiers crucified Christ, her body flinched with each horrendous hammer blow. She stood as near to the cross as the soldiers would allow. Her eyes stared up at the bloodied form of her Lord, but it all seemed so unreal, so impossible. She fought back waves of nausea. The hope that Christ had awakened within her was on that cross. Her entire future hung there, struggling for air. Her faith bled there, too, drop by disastrous drop.

When Christ finally died, Mary's whole body shivered with cold.

The hardest thing I ever did as a pastor started with a phone call at 1:00 A.M. "Pastor, I'm here at the emergency room with my wife. She had a blood clot. Don't bother coming down. We're OK. I just wanted to let you know and ask for your prayers." Something told me to rush down there. When I arrived, the situation had deteriorated terribly. The husband looked very distraught. He only said, "They're giving her CPR." I sat next to him, and we waited. After fifteen minutes, the doctor told us she had died.

The husband asked if I would tell his daughter the awful news in person while he cared for his younger son. His daughter attended college about two hours away. I had two of their close friends, a husband and wife, accompany me. We arrived about six that morning at the dorm. The dean phoned her room and asked her to come to the office. When she walked through the door and saw us, her eyes darted anxiously from person to person, trying to read our faces.

"Cindy," I began, "your mother was taken to the emergency room early this morning." I tried hard to talk very deliberately in spite of my racing heart. "She had a blood clot go to her lungs. They did everything they could at the hospital . . . but she didn't make it."

At first Cindy let out a short, high-pitched squeal and put her hands over her mouth. Her eyes pleaded with me to say it wasn't true. When I offered a pathetically inadequate, "I'm so sorry," she shook her head repeatedly and screamed, "No, no, no." Within moments she collapsed into the arms of those who had come with me.

The wife held her tightly. Cindy's shoulders shook. She whimpered like a fevered child, then broke into body-racking sobs.

That is how I picture Mary Magdalene's initial reaction to the death of Jesus.

Poor Mary sat on the hard ground and hugged herself, rocking back and forth and wailing in pain. As others filtered away, she remained, with her head bowed, whispering Jesus' name over and over. After some time, she looked up and fixed her gaze on Christ's face. His head had slumped down onto His chest, and His eyes were open but unmoving, making it seem as though He were staring in shock at the wounds on His own feet.

When the soldiers came to break the victim's legs, Mary's heart shuddered. "Can't you see that He's already dead!" she shouted and sobbed at the same time. "Can't you see what you've done! Can't you see!" When a spear was shoved into Jesus' side, she had to look away.

As the Savior's body was taken down from the cross and washed, Mary watched every action intently. Later, at the cemetery, she waited until Joseph, Nicodemus, and John had completed the burial. She then drew near, bent down, and repeatedly ran her trembling fingers over the chiseled edges of the large circular stone.

---

[1] *The Desire of Ages,* p. 566.

[2] *The Seventh-day Adventist Bible Commentary,* 5:763.

[3] Ellen G. White, *The Signs of the Times,* 9 May 1900, "At Simon's House."

[4] Patty Derosier Barnes, *The Woman Inside: From Incest Victim to Survivor* (Racine, Wis.: Mother Courage Press, 1989), p. 12.

[5] Carol Poston and Karen Lison, *Reclaiming Our Lives: Hope for Adult Survivors of Incest* (Boston: Little, Brown, 1989), p. 22.

[6] *The Seventh-day Adventist Bible Commentary,* 5:762, 763.

[7] Susan Forward and Craig Buck, *Betrayal of Innocence and Its Devastation* (New York: Penguin, 1978), pp. 21, 22.

[8] *Reclaiming Our Lives: Hope for Adult Survivors of Incest,* p. 127.

[9] *The Woman Inside: From Incest Victim to Survivor,* p. 11.

[10] *The Seventh-day Adventist Bible Commentary,* 5:762.

[11] Emil G. Kraeling, *Bible Atlas* (New York: Rand McNally, 1956), p. 255; and James B. Pritchard et al, *Everyday Life in Bible Times* (Washington D.C.: National Geographic Society, 1967), p. 302.

[12] Jack Finegan, *The Archeology of the New Testament* (Princeton, N.J.: Princeton University Press, 1969), p. 46.

[13] *Everyday Life in Bible Times,* p. 335.

[14] *The Archeology of the New Testament,* p. 46.

[15] Rev. Selah Merrill, *Galilee in the Time of Christ* (London: The Religious Tract Society, 1891), 3rd ed., p. 46.

[16] *Jewish Encyclopedia* (New York: Funk and Wagnalls, 1904), 8:249; *Everyday Life in Bible Times.*

[17] David Noel Freedman, *The Anchor Bible Dictionary* (New York: Doubleday, 1992), 4:579.

[18] *The New English Bible* (London: Oxford University Press and Cambridge University Press, 1970), p. 81.

[19] Eugene H. Peterson, *The Message* (Colorado Springs, Colo.: Navpress, 1993), p. 135.

[20] *The Layman's Parallel New Testament, Living New Testament* (Grand Rapids, Mich.: Zondervan, 1970), p. 223.

[21] William Barclay, *The Gospel of Luke* (Philadelphia: Westminster Press, 1975), p. 95. See also Alfred Plummer, *A Critical and Exegetical Commentary on the Gospel According to St. Luke* (Edinburgh: T. & T. Clark, 1922) 5th ed, p. 210; *The Interpreter's Bible* (New York: Abingdon-Cokesbury, 1952), 8:142; I. Howard Marshall, *The Gospel of Luke: A Commentary on the Greek Text* (Grand Rapids, Mich.: Paternoster Press, 1978), p. 304; Leon Morris, *The Gospel According to St. Luke* (Grand Rapids, Mich.: Eerdmans, 1974), p. 146; Eduard Schweizer, *The Good News According to Luke* (Atlanta: John Knox Press, 1984), p. 139; Norval Geldenhuys, *Commentary on the Gospel of Luke* (Grand Rapids, Mich.: Eerdmans, 1975), p. 237.

[22] *The Anchor Bible Dictionary*, 5:511.

[23] Allen C. Myers, ed., *The Eerdmans Bible Dictionary* (Grand Rapids, Mich.: Eerdmans, 1987), p. 462.

[24] *The Anchor Bible Dictionary*, 5:511.

[25] *Reclaiming Our Lives: Hope for Adult Survivors of Incest*, p. 27.

[26] Elaine Landau, *On The Street: The Lives of Adolescent Prostitutes* (New York: Julian Messner, 1987), p. 37.

[27] Ibid., pp. 89, 90.

[28] Ibid., p. 4.

[29] *The Seventh-day Adventist Bible Commentary*, 5:765.

[30] *The Anchor Bible Dictionary*, 4:579.

[31] *Everyday Life in Bible Times*, p. 342; *The Seventh-day Adventist Bible Commentary*, 5:322.

[32] *On The Street: The Lives of Adolescent Prostitutes*, p. 58.

[33] *The Desire of Ages*, p. 568.

[34] Ibid.

[35] *The Seventh-day Adventist Bible Commentary*, 5:765.

[36] Ibid., 5:197, 198.

[37] *The Anchor Bible Dictionary*, 4:579.

[38] *The Seventh-day Adventist Bible Commentary*, 5:766 and *The New Interpreter's Bible* (Nashville: Abingdon, 1995), 9:170.

[39] *The Gospel According to Matthew*, p. 647.

[40] *The Gospel According to John*, p. 576.

[41] *The Seventh-day Adventist Bible Commentary*, 5:762.

[42] Ibid., 5:619, 620.

[43] Ibid., p. 518.

[44] *The Interpreter's Dictionary of the Bible* (Nashville: Abingdon, 1962), p. 932; *The Anchor Bible Dictionary*, 5:507.

[45] *The Desire of Ages*, p. 559.

[46] *Reclaiming Our Lives: Hope for Adult Survivors of Incest*, p. 204.

Chapter 4

The Greatest Miracle

Shafts of light from Friday's setting sun sped across vast stretches of empty universe, past planets and asteroids, through earth's layered atmosphere, only to be halted three yards from their Creator. They were blocked by a seven-inch-thick stone rolled across the entrance to Jesus' tomb. The barrier was designed to keep out thieves and famished animals desperate enough to munch on a bandaged corpse. The few bits of light that did manage to wriggle past the outer edges of the uneven stone kept the darkness within from being absolute.

Christ's battered body was about to spend its first full night in the isolated, eerie confines of Joseph's brand new tomb. As the sun finally disappeared below the horizon, the interior of the tomb descended into total blackness.

The thought of such inky darkness takes me back to the aged house our family inhabited for most of my growing-up years. At night it creaked and groaned like a multi-gabled, hilltop residence in a stomach-churning horror film. Until the birth of my younger sister, I was always the first to bed, between 8:00 and 9:00 P.M. No matter how gingerly I placed my feet, each stairstep moaned like a disembodied spirit.

At the top of the stairs there was a wide rectangular landing. I knew full well that the bathroom on the right would be a perfect hiding place for a deranged kidnapper. With one swoop of his hairy, heavily tattooed arm, he could snatch me up, gag me, drag me out through the oversized window, force me down the trellis to an awaiting get-away car, and sell me on the black market for unvigilant kids.

The entrance to my bedroom was a few steps to the left. The hallway light created odd shapes and shadows within that seemed to call out, "Come in here, little boy. We promise not to harm you. Ha, ha, ha." The distance from the doorway to my bed was only about ten feet, but I never simply walked over to the bed and climbed in. That would be the height of juvenile folly. Underneath, there existed an invisible, primeval world of unspeakable things. I usually started running about mid-hallway, flew into the room, and leaped the final treacherous four feet. Once on the bed, the universal rule for the preservation of body parts was, "Don't let anything you care about dangle over the edge!"

Biblically, darkness is often a metaphor for evil. Even in society at large, darkness conjures up images of crime, muggings, vandalism, rape, and violence done in the anonymity of night. We talk about the "forces of darkness" that intend us harm. We feel far more vulnerable in the dark and instinctively become more wary.

The Light of the world entered a place of thick darkness two thousand years ago, a cold, forbidding place designed to harbor death. By way of analogy, imagine your own dead body, dressed up in your favorite outfit from the mall, being placed in a coffin. Your lifeless head is carefully positioned on a starkly white, silken pillow, your arms folded, legs straight.

The funeral director expertly closes and locks the lid. Your coffin is lowered into a rectangular hole and buried under six feet of freshly disturbed dirt. Friends and relatives filter away from the scene in tears, leaving you outdoors, alone, in a field that is home to other dead people in various stages of unhappy decomposition. That is essentially what Christ let happen to Himself as they closed Joseph's tomb, and the setting sun withdrew its reassuring rays. The Author of life voluntarily entered the hellish, dust-to-dust confines of death. Like a soldier killed in war, the Son of God was buried far from home on the field of battle.

Inside Jesus' cavelike grave, various smells blended and co-existed—damp moss, musky dirt, musty lichen. Small dots of mouse dung collected in favorite corners. Moth wings made minuscule ripples in the deathly still atmosphere. As the night temperature dropped, the terrain contracted. Mother Earth rearranged herself, creaking inward to conserve heat. Drops of water from a distant spring hit the stone floor of the man-made tomb with the regularity of a drumbeat. If you sat exactly still, you could hear a faint whistling sound as gusts of wind blew across a slight opening in the surface. A wild dog sniffed and scratched at the entrance. The Son of God lay on His narrow shelf, stiff and cold.

After the mourners left, the bugs took charge of the corpse. Two spiders crept under the linen napkin around Jesus' head. One walked across His ridged lips, along the bruised nose, over the left eyelid and onto His broad forehead, disappearing somewhere in stiff, matted clumps of hair. The other spider traversed the right cheekbone, settled in the Savior's ear, and started to spin. Ants began, here and there, to probe the outer layer of linen wrappings.

Our Lord's corpse cooled approximately one and a half degrees an hour until it reached the temperature of the tomb itself. The cooling was most rapid in the outer layers of skin and worked its way into the body's core.[1]

Rigor mortis started about three hours after Jesus' death, as glycogen in His cells was converted into lactic acid.[2] This stiffening of the body affected the small muscles around the face and eyelids first then eventually worked its way into the larger muscle groups.

Livor mortis, which literally means "the color of death," is a growing discoloration of the skin caused by the settling of the blood once circulation ceases.[3] Gravity pulls the blood downward. Between one and four hours after Christ died, reddish-purple blotches appeared on the underside of His body. After six to eight hours the blotches began to merge.

This was the first Friday evening the Savior couldn't gaze up at the stars or take in a deep, invigorating draft of fresh night air. It was the first Sabbath He couldn't stroll the moonlit shore of the Sea of Galilee. The first Sabbath He couldn't pray to His Father in heaven or sing praises from the Psalms. The first Sabbath in recent memory that He couldn't gather His disciples around and assure them of His love.

Outside the tomb, in the city of Jerusalem, priests blew sacred trumpets. Thousands of worshippers pressed into the temple area, eager for a blessing. A huge choir dressed in sacred robes praised God in song. Large offerings were collected and little lambs sacrificed as church life continued, on time and unabated. Murdering God didn't hamper most people's religious zeal.[4]

The only significant interruption in the Passover festivities came from the hundreds of sick people gathered near the Court of the Gentiles on Saturday morning. In my imagination, I see a man named Melkana, who was caught up in the milling mass of pain and suffering.[5] As he wiped his worried forehead, he glanced back at his gravely ill wife, who lay in a small cart pulled by the family's lone donkey. They had traveled together for two weeks seeking a miracle.

Her condition was deteriorating rapidly. Death seemed very near. Melkana bent down, lifted his wife's fevered head, and poured small amounts of water onto her scabbed-over lips. She coughed severely as the liquid spilled down her ulcerated throat. Looking around at no one in particular, her husband yelled anxiously, "We need to see Jesus right away! Can anyone tell me where to find Jesus?"

He looked down at his beloved wife again, and tears welled up in his eyes as he thought, *We've come so far. I can't let her die so near help.* His mind flashed back to the hopeful look on the faces of their two small children when they promised to pray faithfully for Mommy as he left them at a relative's home.

"I beg you to tell me where I can find Jesus!" Melkana yelled again.

As he scanned the crowd, he saw a violent fight break out near the gate leading into the temple area. Friends and relatives of the sick and dying demanded entrance, searching for the Miracle Worker from Nazareth. The Jewish authorities adamantly refused to permit such bleeding, stinking, unclean worshippers to contaminate the sacred precincts.

Suddenly Roman soldiers rode into the seething throng, forcing people back with swords, herding them like cattle, yelling obscenities. "Go home, you fools!" an officer cried out. "Your Healer is dead, dead as those stones over there! We crucified your Messiah yesterday. Go home, all of you!" Heavily armed foot soldiers poured into the area. The Jewish priests had frantically called in the riot police to restore order.[6]

Melkana found himself caught up in a moving crush of humanity. People stepped on one another. Elbows flailed. Blood-curdling yells pierced the air. Melkana was barely able to catch the reigns of his donkey and get the cart pulled around in the growing panic. As he strained forward, he saw the crowd open in horror around a disfigured leper clad in frayed rags. The pathetic man lay on the ground, covering his head with his arms, yelling hoarsely for Christ.[7]

As Melkana hurriedly guided his cart down a road away from the eastern gate of the city, he cast worried glances back at his wife. When the dangerous crowd finally thinned, he pulled off to the side of the road. He rushed to tend to his wife's withered form, but she had already stopped breathing. Melkana sank to his knees and wept.

Back within the city, during the Saturday Sabbath, several of Jesus' disciples gathered in the upper room of Mark's home. Some of them sat in shock and grief-stricken silence. Others recounted the horrible events of the previous day, needing to talk out their bewilderment and pain. Finger pointing and blame erupted. Everyone's hopes and dreams lay in ruins. The bright future had turned to dust.

James deliberately sat in the same place he occupied at the Last Supper. He looked over at the head of the table where Christ had so recently reclined. The words spoken that night came back to the heartbroken disciple with renewed force. Oh, how he longed to hear his Master's reassuring voice once again.

Saturday afternoon the distinctive clink of armor and the rhythmic tread of military feet marked the arrival of a hundred Roman soldiers around Jesus' grave.[8] Just outside the entrance a centurion barked out orders. "Bring up that rope and the wax. You four men secure these cords across the stone and seal it. There won't be any body-snatching during my watch." The Jewish priests had devised this creative way of making the tomb tamper proof. It was the first-century version of a modern-day alarm system.

"Sixty of you position yourselves in a perimeter about twenty-five yards out," the centurion continued. "The other forty men I want right here near the grave. Stay alert, all of you! If anyone suspicious shows up, use deadly force."

The soldiers settled in for their odd two-day mission. These were some of the same men-in-arms who mocked Christ in the Praetorium and crowned Him with cruel thorns.[9] As the evening wore on, they traded stories about their latest exploits with women and groused about the absurdity of their assignment. "I thought we were done with this joker yesterday. Rome won't be handing out any medals for keeping a dead man in his grave. This whole thing is crazy if you ask me."

Fully outfitted in a bronze helmet, segmented body armor, leather sandals, and red military cloak, the soldier on the left of the tomb entrance wrapped his thick fingers around a shield in one hand and a "gladius" or short sword in the other.[10] His heavily-haired, tree trunk–sized legs supported a hulking upper torso capped by broad shoulders and a square-jawed head. Multiple facial scars testified to his courage. Another veteran soldier stood guard like a bookend to the right.

Evil angels also surrounded the tomb.[11] At Calvary, Satan had hoped to defeat Christ spiritually and emerge as victor. But having utterly failed on Golgotha, the evil one now desperately wanted to keep the Son of God in the grave, to seal Him inside His rock cell forever.[12]

Satan had a vast army at his disposal. Eons before, fully one third of all the angels God created had joined the devil's ranks. How the Trinity must have grieved to see millions and millions of beings They loved side with the rebel leader. Those same mighty angels eagerly rallied around Satan's audacious plan. The evil one called as many of his minions as possible from their duties around the globe to take part in this crucial assignment. Satan had been completely humiliated at Calvary, and his heart now burned with renewed hatred and revenge.

The devil rallied his forces with an impassioned speech. He concluded by saying, "The Son of God can now suffer the same fate as the rest of us if we stand our ground. I don't ever want to see His miserable face again. At all costs you must keep Him in that tomb!"

Satan then told his leaders how to position the immense angelic army and keep any heavenly rescuers at bay. I picture the devil setting up a multi-layered defense, utilizing several million evil angels to cover an area up to five thousand miles above the earth. "I'm counting on you!" he said. "We're not going to make the same mistake we did in heaven during the 'Great War' when this noble rebellion began." He also deployed part of his forces at the tomb itself.

Holy angels of immense strength faithfully guarded Jesus' grave. Their orders were clear. "Keep the Lord safe from the wiles of the devil. Make sure that the eternal plan is fully carried out."

The most powerful forces in heaven and earth gathered about this crucial, unassuming graveyard. The stage was set for a momentous showdown. Spiritual forces faced each other with might and weaponry that humans cannot comprehend. As the hours ticked slowly by, the eyes of countless beings throughout the universe were riveted on the Judean cave and its murdered Occupant. Satan took up a position about ten thousand miles above the earth. He nervously stared into outer space, waiting and wondering.

Christ's throne in heaven remained empty. His crown lay to one side. Saturday evening God the Father called Gabriel to His side to review the next day's decisive events. The angelic choir also met to rehearse again for tomorrow's unprecedented celebration. Unfallen beings from around the cosmos began to arrive in heaven. Everyone kept checking their watches.

Inside the tomb, only small, unassuming events marked the snaillike passage of time.

• *7:05 P.M., Saturday*—the last bits of light that had filtered past the entrance stone withdrew, and complete blackness took over the night shift.

• *8:23 P.M., Saturday*—a corner cobweb was spun further until it reached out like a thin gossamer vine.

• *9:16 P.M., Saturday*—an uncertain, newly formed, half-inch-long, black beetle meandered across the bumpy mausoleum floor like a teenager taking his first driving lesson.

• *9:58 P.M., Saturday*—a dark-green patch of lichen spread upward another tenth of a millimeter on the inner northwest wall.

• *11:34 P.M., Saturday*—a small, striped snake, trapped inside the cave, curled up more tightly.

• *12:07 A.M., Sunday*—a long, feathery root added a few more cells to its silken tendrils.

• *2:47 A.M., Sunday*—an ant compulsively cleaned its antennae.

• *3:51 A.M., Sunday*—the earth moaned as it waited impatiently for someone to release its lifeless Resident.

At 4:41 Sunday morning, just before dawn, a flash of light overhead caused Satan to quickly look up. Within moments, he realized that it was the angel Gabriel descending toward earth. The devil shouted anxiously at his followers to resist.

Immense shock waves preceded Gabriel's approach. (See Matthew 28:2.) Ear-splitting thunder boomed throughout the heavens. Long, jagged shafts of light shot across the sky as he carried out his remarkable, single-handed assault on the enemy positions. The evil one's imposing defenses braced for combat, tracking Gabriel every microsecond. With great precision they let loose an astonishing barrage of firepower.

Satan watched in horror as God's head angel sliced through his forces like a sword through an overripe pomegranate. As Gabriel neared the earth, he became engulfed in bright, reddish-orange flame, like a space vehicle burning its way through the atmosphere.[13] At the tomb, every single evil angel fled in abject terror. Satan was beside himself with rage as he watched his followers scatter like roaches in the sunlight.[14]

Gabriel's tumultuous arrival created a severe earthquake. One of the soldiers at the tomb was walking toward his woolen bedroll, when the earth convulsed violently under his feet like a dog shaking off water. Instantly he fell onto his battle-tested backside. All the other men-in-arms were tossed into heaps.[15]

Inside the tomb, pieces of stone and dust shook loose and showered onto the floor. Jesus' tightly bandaged body rocked back and forth on its narrow, undulating shelf. As seen from inside the grave, the angel's radiance caused the inner edges of the circular entrance to burst into a halo of light like the shimmering corona of a solar eclipse.

The large stone designed to seal in the Lord of the universe was rolled to the right. Someone has rightly commented that the angel removed the stone not to permit Christ to come out but to enable the disciples later to go in.[16] Gabriel's glory filled the inside of the cave with crisscrossing, laserlike white, green, and golden rays.

Another angel eagerly entered the tomb and tore open the Savior's bandages. At the pinnacle of this immense, pivotal drama, Gabriel called from outside with the voice of great authority, "Son of God, come forth; Thy Father calls Thee!"

Throughout the universe, heavenly beings held their collective breath. The devil and his evil spirits stared at the grave with throat-constricting nervousness.

Jesus' body began to stir. His head moved slightly. The toes and fingers twitched. Muscles, veins, arteries, vital organs, every single incarnated cell surged with everlasting, irreversible, resurrection life. His eyes opened and adjusted.

Christ turned, looked at the opening to the outside and smiled. His legs swung around. He leaned forward, stood upright, joyfully hugged the angel standing nearby, and paused to carefully fold the burial wrappings. The Lord of the universe then bent low and made His way out into the dazzling light.

As Christ stepped into the garden graveyard, the heavenly angels burst into anthems of victory and praise. Trumpets blared impossibly high notes. The Son of God glowed more brightly than at the Transfiguration, causing every tree, shrub, and leaf near the tomb to shimmer in reflected brilliance. Shafts of lightning turned the sky into a massive grid of kaleidoscopic flame. Thunder like the roar of volcanic explosions rumbled across Judea. The earth reeled under Jesus' tread.

The repercussions from the tumult at the tomb could be felt throughout the region. [17] On the surrounding hills huge boulders broke loose and rolled violently down the grassy slopes.[18] Hundreds of startled sparrows, doves, and ravens flew up from the trees. Donkeys brayed and strained at their tethers. Sheep scrambled randomly in fear. Wolves and jackals fled. In the city, panicked residents gathered family members and ran into the streets.

A sixty-seven-year-old widow in a quiet rural village twelve miles from Jerusalem instinctively clutched the sides of her bed as her little brick home shook and trembled. She could hear the clay cooking pots tumble off the wooden shelf near the window, smashing onto the dirt floor. Just two days before, about 3:00 P.M. Friday afternoon, another set of pots had crashed down during a similar earthquake. She swore then screamed for her brother.

Above the din, Jesus' rich tenor voice rang out in clear, penetrating tones. "I am the Resurrection and the Life!" Trees in the garden leaned backward from the force of His powerful pronouncement. Throughout the galaxies, billions of unfallen beings hugged each other and cheered. Every eye in heaven shed tears of joy. God the Father sang.

Earlier in His ministry Christ had declared, " 'No one takes [my life] from me, but I lay it down of my own accord. I have power to lay it down, and I have power to take it again' " (John 10:18). He possessed two types of power, one to *allow,* the other to *take.*

Regarding His death, Jesus, in effect, said, "Caiaphas, I know you think you have the authority to vote My condemnation, but it will only be because I let you. Pilate, I know you think you can consign me to the cross, but only because I willingly consent. Mr. Roman Centurion, I know you think you are in charge of My untimely death, but only because I *allow* it to be so. Believe Me, nothing will happen this Friday without My full knowledge and consent."

Then, Sunday morning, the Son of God essentially announced, "I will now *take* back My life, and no evil angels, no soldiers, no stone, no wrappings, not even death itself can keep Me one second longer in this wretched grave. God calls Me, and I must be about My Father's business."[19] "Mountains piled upon mountains over His sepulcher could not have prevented Him from coming forth."[20]

After the Resurrection, the Son of God walked into an open field of delicate blue wildflowers to pray. A handful of thick cumulus clouds floated across the early morning sky. Gusts of wind whipped His glowing white robe and tossed His long brown hair. Jesus took in several deep drafts of dew-moistened air, then made His way back near the tomb.

When He had consoled Mary Magdalene, He disappeared from view and ascended quickly to His Father. The Son of God traversed trillions and trillions of miles in mere seconds, past asteroids, planets, quasars, black holes, neutron stars, and countless galaxies. When He arrived in heaven, He flew through a living corridor of righteous angels that opened onto the center of the Holy City. The angels bowed deeply as the Lord passed by.

The Savior touched down gently and walked through a series of glimmering archways toward the vast, breathtaking throne room of the universe, bigger than scores of astrodomes or skydomes. Inside, the Father sat upon a high, regal throne enshrouded in an immense, intensely bright, pulsating, white light. A breathtaking rainbow half a mile wide arched overhead.

Within moments, the Son of God stood framed in the doorway. A hush fell over all in attendance. The Light on the throne rose and moved forward. Christ strode quickly on. Soon, He and the Father embraced, lingering together. Jesus then stepped back slightly and declared, "Father, I present to You My life, My suffering, and death, as an atonement for sinful man as the fulfillment of Our covenant."

God the Father declared the unforgettable words: "Your great sacrifice, My Son, is more than sufficient. I declare that all who believe in You may now be given eternal life and join the family of heaven forever."[21]

---

[1] Web site: www.astolat.demon.co.uk/forensic/bodies.htm.

[2] We bsite: www.astolat.demon.co.uk/forensic/bodies/htm.

[3] Web sites: www.astolat.demon.co.uk/forensic/bodies/htm and www.yossarian.com/forensic/livor.shtml.

[4] *The Desire of Ages,* p. 774.

[5] Based on *The Desire of Ages,* p. 776.

[6] See *The Desire of Ages,* p. 776.

[7] *The Desire of Ages,* p. 776.

[8] Ibid., p. 778.
[9] Ibid., p. 780.
[10] Web site: http://myron.sjsu.edu/romeweb/ROMARMY/equip.htm.
[11] *The Desire of Ages,* p. 779.
[12] Ibid., p. 782.
[13] Ibid., p. 779.
[14] Ibid., p. 782.
[15] Ibid., pp. 780, 781.
[16] G. D. Yarnold, *Risen Indeed* (London: Oxford University Press, 1959), p. 24.
[17] *The Desire of Ages,* p. 780.
[18] Ibid.
[19] Ibid., p. 785.
[20] Ibid., p. 781.
[21] *The Desire of Ages,* p. 790.

Chapter 5

The Women First

Resurrection Sunday had to be the best day of Jesus' life. He longed to turn the grief of His closest companions into extraordinary joy. He had spent three years with this motley band of disciples and was anxious to dispel their confusion and despair. After He rose from the grave, He pictured each one in His mind and smiled as He anticipated their upcoming reaction to the incredible news He was about to share.

The greatest personal news I have ever shared was the birth of our daughter, Stefanie. My parents had no grandchildren yet, and I knew how ecstatic they would be when I phoned them with the announcement.

Our precious baby came into this world at the convenient hour of 4:00 A.M. After she was safely whisked away to the nursery and my wife eased her death grip on my left hand, I made a beeline for the nearest pay phone. My heart was pounding. As I dialed, I anticipated Mom's shout of glee.

After eight rings, a sleepy voice on the other end spoke an unsteady, "Hello?"

"It's a girl!" I shouted. "We just had a wonderful baby girl!"

There was a pause and then the person answered, "A what? Who is this?"

In my eagerness I had dialed the wrong number.

"Sorry," I offered sheepishly and took a moment to explain.

"No problem," the unwitting celebrant replied, "and congratulations!"

Nice guy. I carefully dialed again, made my announcement, and heard the hoped-for scream of delight on the other end.

Likewise, Christ longed to share the wonderful, life-changing announcement of His own resurrection. The Savior would remain physically present with His followers until their doubts turned to certainty and their cowardice turned to courage.

Jesus made a total of ten post-Resurrection appearances—five on Resurrection Sunday and five more spread out over the next forty days. These meetings were primarily designed to help His followers comprehend certain vital truths so that the fledgling movement could take root and grow.

First, the Lord wanted His followers to understand that He was not a spirit but had risen in a real human body and was the same Jesus they had always known so well.

Second, that His intense love for them was undiminished in spite of their desertion in the Garden and subsequent faithlessness.

Third, that His mission was foretold and explained in the Old Testament scriptures.

Fourth, that His death and resurrection made salvation available to all sinners.

Fifth, that the Resurrection was Heaven's stamp of approval on what He had taught about the kingdom of heaven. His kingdom had nothing to do with military might but was characterized by servanthood, grace, and unconditional love.

Sixth, that His resurrection now made it possible for them to become an unstoppable, worldwide movement through the power of the Holy Spirit.

Each of the appearances was like a classroom where Christ could talk about one or more of these truths. Although the ten appearances were separate events, they were nonetheless closely linked as the building blocks of a new vision and understanding.

The Savior could have written the news of His resurrection across the sky in gigantic fiery letters. He could have called upon the immense angelic choir to sing the stunning announcement in soaring melodies that rang throughout the heavens. Instead, He entrusted that universe-altering message to a tiny handful of stammering sinners.

Appearance to Mary Magdalene

Sabbath had been a long, cruel day for Mary Magdalene. On Saturday, the leftover sense of shock from Friday's awful events seeped more fully into her consciousness, leaving her physically and emotionally drained. She used herbs and warm water to ease her pounding headache. The screams of the mob and the hammer blows on Golgotha kept ringing in her ears. All night she tossed restlessly in bed.

Very early Sunday morning, Mary quietly stepped outside into the predawn darkness. She had anointed Christ at Simon's home before His death and planned now to anoint Him a second time at the tomb. She had no idea how she was going to remove the huge stone from the entrance, but love that is hurting does not calculate.

Nearing the place of burial, she felt the ground shake violently and saw a burst of sun-bright light in the distance. Losing her balance, she dropped to her knees and reached out to keep herself from falling over. Jesus' intrepid follower stared in anxious amazement at the eerie radiance pulsating through the trees. Soon the light faded, and she sat down on the stony pathway for several minutes, trying to regain her composure. Part of her wanted to run, but she chose instead to get up and cautiously move forward. Mary didn't realize that she had just witnessed from afar the resurrection of her Lord.[1]

When she arrived at the graveside, she was shocked to find the tomb open and concluded that Jesus' body must have been stolen.[2] (See John 20:1, 2.) What an unnerving discovery that must have been.

On August 28, 2000, my dad died after a lingering illness. My siblings and I took the tearful casket tour at the local funeral home and chose a mid-priced, walnut-colored coffin. Believe me, I would have been stunned if three days after the graveside ceremony I returned and found everything dug up and that casket wide open and empty. An awful sense of violation would sweep over me. I'd be thinking malicious vandalism, not resurrection. Wouldn't you?

And it was that same sense of alarm and fright that swirled within the heart of Mary as she stood wide-eyed and incredulous at the vacant tomb. She gasped, dropped her bag of spices, and fled to find Peter and John.

After Mary told the disciples about the body-less tomb, impulsive Peter immediately charged out the door, retracing Mary's steps. John left after him, but his youthful legs pumped past Peter, and he arrived at the grave first. Hesitant, the young disciple knelt down on all fours, squinted, and looked into the dark, shadow-etched interior. Peter arrived moments later, elbowed his partner aside, and practically dove inside the tomb. Gathering his courage, John followed.

As their eyes adjusted in the dim light, they could see Jesus' grave clothes laid out as neatly as if some cemetery maid had just finished tidying up.[3] (See John 20:6, 7.) Those unoccupied wrappings were left behind as beyond-reasonable-doubt clues for open hearts.

Suddenly, something clicked in John's racing mind. *No grave robber would take the time to unwrap and fold the linen,* he thought. And right there, standing in death's local headquarters, hope pressed through the word *impossible,* and he believed. At that point, his faith in the Resurrection must not have been firm enough to try and persuade others, but the seeds of understanding began to germinate. With mixed emotions, Peter and John hurried away.

Mary Magdalene now returned mournfully to the tomb for the second time. Her love required answers. She had to find the body of her Lord.

Preoccupied with her pain, Mary knelt down, pulled her shawl up to her face and wept. She leaned forward, peered into the tomb, and saw two angels in human form. They asked why she was crying, and she replied, " 'Because they have taken away my Lord, and I do not know where they have laid him' " (John 20:13).

In the Jewish culture of that day any disrespect shown to a corpse was abhorrent. The obvious desecration of Jesus' body, plus the uncertainty about where it had been taken, troubled her greatly.[4] Morton Kelsey observes, "Not being able to perform the last ritual was the end of the road, the last indignity, a final stab at her heart. No wonder she wept."[5]

Jesus approached quietly from behind and looked down at His crestfallen follower. His great heart went out to her. Years before, she had been so terribly wronged by Simon and endured such deep, corrosive hurt in Magdala. How desperately she had sought healing. How brave she had been to return home to Bethany, to face malicious gossip and glances of contempt from townspeople. Though ostracized by local Jewish leaders, she remained faithful to the Savior and grew to love Him more and more. Not even His death could dim her fierce loyalty.

Christ spoke gently, " 'Why are you weeping? Whom do you seek?' " (John 20:15). She turned but saw Him only indistinctly through a flood of tears.

I can identify somewhat with Mary's hazy, tear-blurred vision. About two and half years ago I was sitting in the congregation during Sabbath worship when a deacon tapped me on the shoulder and whispered urgently, "There's a phone call for you." My heart skipped a beat because a phone call at that place, at that hour, could not be good news.

I put the phone to my ear. "This is Kim Johnson," I offered nervously.

A nearly hysterical voice shouted, "He's dead, Michael's dead!"

My mind struggled to comprehend what I was hearing. How could it be? How could such a thing happen to someone so young?

Michael and I had been working together in adjoining offices for years. During that time we became soul mates, kindred spirits, sharing our inmost thoughts and feelings.

At first I faced his tragic, untimely death stoically, ignoring my own grief in an attempt to uplift others. But when I returned to work two days after the funeral, I couldn't maintain my composure any longer.

Entering my office, I saw Michael's desk just beyond an open doorway. I dreaded going into his room, but forced myself nonetheless. After several trudging steps forward, my attention was drawn to the mosaic of Garfield cartoons still covering his bulletin board. To the left lay the desk calendar and familiar handwriting. On a side table sat the Macintosh computer he loved. I just stood there and wept.

Turning to leave, I could barely make out the form of someone standing directly in front of me. After wiping my eyes with the back of a sleeve, I offered a tentative "Hello?" to whoever was there.

"Hard day, my brother," a voice responded.

After blinking back more tears, I inquired, "Jim? Is that you, Jim?" Anticipating my plight, two deeply caring mutual friends had driven a couple of hours early in the morning to be with me in my moment of need. I hugged them both and said, "I didn't realize it was you. I'm so glad that you came."

Mary, blinded by tears, saw the blurred form of Someone standing next to her and pleaded, "Sir, if you've taken my Master's body, please let me know where you've laid Him. I'm not in a position to be making any demands, but please, sir, I've got to see Him one more time. Is that too much to ask? If there is even a shred of decency left in this world, I beg you to tell me where to find Him."

Her voice broke as she continued, "I'll make a bargain, sir. If this tomb is too good for my Jesus, if that's the problem, I'll find some way to bury Him myself in the grave my brother occupied only two months ago. Oh, please help me." She buried her head in her hands and cried some more.

Christ paused to wipe the tears from His own eyes then spoke to His intrepid follower again with immense compassion. This time He simply said, "Mary."

Something in the way He spoke her name caught her attention.[6] The tone was unmistakable.[7] Instantly, "she recognized his voice. Jesus had spoken that name with warmth and care when others spoke it only with scorn and derision."[8]

Mary turned, looked up into the face of Jesus, and screamed, "Rabboni!!" She lunged forward and grasped His feet in adoration just as she had at Simon's feast. She longed to hold Him tightly so He would never be lost to her again.

The word *rabboni* can be translated not only as "my master" but also much more personally as "my *dear* master."[9] The King James rendering of Christ's response in John 20:17, "Touch me not," is inaccurate. It should really read, " 'Do not hold me,' " (RSV) or " ' "Do not cling to me" ' " (NEB). The problem was that she would not let Him go.[10] Christ was saying, "Mary, you don't need to grasp onto to Me so desperately. Nothing can hurt Me anymore." Clutching someone's feet could also be a form of worship, and Jesus couldn't accept such homage until His sacrifice had been openly endorsed by the Father.

Soon Christ disappeared from Mary's view, but how her heart sang! "She knew that he was the teacher, the master, the lord, the conqueror, God. She had been right to let that voice break into the sealed fortress of her heart. Meaning and love and hope were real. People did not just use one another. The universe did not just use people and cast them off. What a beautiful morning it was! The flowers were blooming in the garden, primroses and wild lilies, roses, red and white; she was as alive as they were. The world was green and new."[11]

Appearance to the "other women"

Mary Magdalene had been the first at the tomb. After she left to find Peter and John, the "other women" arrived who were supposed to join her earlier. This group of mourners included Mary the mother of James and Joses, Salome, and Joanna. (See Mark 16:1; Luke 24:10.) Mary the mother of James and Joses was probably the same person as the "other Mary" who had lingered with Mary Magdalene at the tomb after Jesus' burial.[12] (See Mark 15:47; Matthew 27:61.)

Salome was apparently the wife of Zebedee and the mother of the apostles James and John.[13] She had come to Jesus earlier in His ministry asking that her boys be given the two top spots in the new kingdom, once the Romans were eliminated. (See Matthew 20:20-23.) She may also have been the sister of Mary the mother of Jesus.[14]

The Scriptures indicate that Joanna was married to Chuza. (See Luke 8:3.) He held a position of great power and prestige within the court of King Herod, overseeing all of his financial affairs. Somehow Joanna became one of Jesus' main financial backers, often traveling with His entourage. It is a delicious thought that King Herod indirectly subsidized Christ's ministry through this brave woman. Joanna had taken great risks to follow the Savior, probably sacrificing her reputation and high standing in society. Now, the Man on whom she had staked her future was dead. Without regretting her decision to follow Christ, she, along with the others, longed to give Him the best possible burial. [15]

The first thing these women witnessed at the grave was, without doubt, one of the most memorable images of the Resurrection story. The angel that called Jesus forth from the dead was now sitting on top of the stone that had sealed the tomb. (See Matthew 28:2.)[16] He perched on it with his legs dangling and swinging like a schoolboy's. What had been a barrier now became a resting place. By sitting there so casually, the angel was saying, "Death holds no real terror. I can rest here in this cemetery as peacefully as if I were stretched out, chewing straw, on the banks of the river Jordan." His heavenly presence turned a graveyard into a state park.

The angel graciously calmed the women's fears and told them, " 'I know that you seek Jesus *who was crucified*' " (Matthew 28:5, italics supplied). In other words, "I know you came looking for a dead man, a murder victim. I know your minds and hearts are still back at Friday, but this is Sunday, and, believe me, a whole lot has changed."

He then shared one of the huge foundational facts on which Christianity is built: *"He is not here."* A unique aspect of the good news is that it highly values something that was empty, a vacant tomb. No archeological dig would ever consider celebrating such a find.

The most famous tomb story outside of Scripture is probably the discovery of the burial chamber of the Egyptian king Tutankhamen. Howard Carter, the famed British archeologist, was running out of time. Lord Carnarvon had funded Carter's fruitless attempts to find the young king's grave for years and finally decided to pull the plug on the entire expedition. Carter begged for one more season of digging, and Carnarvon reluctantly consented.

On November 4, 1922, after only a few days of searching, the archeological team unearthed the top of a descending stone stairway. Step by step they excavated until the overjoyed Carter stood before a sealed doorway. Upon closer examination, he found the *cartouche* or nameplate of Tutankhamen. The news spread like wildfire.

Beyond the door lay a corridor filled with rocks and rubble. Once that was cleared, they found yet another sealed door. They couldn't tell if the chamber on the other side was intact or if it had been robbed and plundered of all its treasurers as had so many others. A vacant tomb would be a crushing disappointment.

Carter cautiously chiseled a hole in the upper corner of the plaster door and held up a candle. Lord Carnarvon leaned over him and, after what seemed like an eternity, anxiously inquired, "Can you see anything?"

The intrepid explorer replied, "Yes, it is wonderful!"

Carter's journal records, "Our sensations and astonishment are difficult to describe as the better light revealed to us the marvelous collection of treasures."[17] The tomb was filled with more than three thousand priceless artifacts.[18] He later reported what he saw in the chamber called the Treasury. He wrote, "Facing the doorway, on the farther side, stood the most beautiful monument that I have ever seen—so lovely that it made one gasp with wonder and admiration. The central portion of it consisted of a large shrine-shaped chest, completely overlaid with gold."[19] In addition, there were alabaster vases, finely carved chairs, stools, beds, couches, a golden inlaid throne, chariots glittering with gold, statuettes, shrines, jewelry, animal carvings, plus other treasures made with exquisite artistry.

In the burial chamber, they found a large, red quartzite sarcophagus containing three coffins inside of each other. The last coffin, holding Tutankhamen's mummy, was made of solid gold weighing approximately 243 pounds.[20] The most famous find was the king's golden burial mask inlaid with numerous precious stones. It took the archeologists ten years to catalogue, wrap, remove, transport, and preserve all the contents of that glorious tomb.

Two thousand years ago, news about the opening of the tomb of Jesus Christ also spread like wildfire. But in stark contrast to the grave of Tutankhamen, it became world-famous because it was empty. There was nothing in there of any earthly value. As people peered into Christ's burial chamber, the only artifact they could find was some used linen bandages. And yet it is that tomb, and not King Tutankhamen's, that has given hope to millions.

A second angel soon spoke to the spellbound women at the Savior's grave. He and the other holy messenger joyfully told them four separate times that the unimaginable had indeed taken place: (1) " 'He is not here: for He is *risen.*' " (2) " 'Go quickly, and tell His disciples that He is *risen.*' " (3) " 'He is not here, but is *risen.*' " (4) " 'The Son of man must be . . . crucified, and the third day *rise again.*' " [21] (Matthew 28:6, 7; Mark 16:6; Luke 24:6, 7). Bursting with amazing news, Mary the mother of James and Joses, Salome, Joanna, and several other women, raced toward the upper room less than a mile away.

At some point in their short journey, they saw an unusual figure standing in the road ahead of them. He seemed to be staring in their direction. The women stopped, looked at the Man more carefully, and then at each other. The Stranger began walking toward them slowly. Salome wondered whether to run, yet, like the others, remained transfixed. Then, as if with one voice, they all suddenly shouted that it was the Lord.

They ran up and fell down in front of Him, holding on to His feet in a spontaneous act of adoration. The scene was reminiscent of a soldier who had been listed as "Killed in action" returning unannounced to his exultant family.

After conversing briefly with the women, Jesus urged them to go quickly and testify to the disciples about what they had seen. "Go now, I'll see you again. Please tell the others as soon as possible." Their hair and robes flew out behind them as they rushed toward Jerusalem, laughing, reminiscing, sharing hopes and dreams for the future. This astonishing Resurrection day, which minutes earlier held only the prospect of unsavory burial details, had suddenly opened up a lifetime of possibilities.

They banged on the door to the upper room and were let inside. Their excited voices overlapped as they all tried to share the wonderful news simultaneously.

The Scriptures record the disciples' faithless response to the women's report: "But these words seemed to them an idle tale, and they did not believe them" (Luke 24:11). The words translated "idle tale" are the same as those used in medical language of the day to describe " ' "the wild talk of the sick in de-lirium." ' "[22] The men thought these women were out of their minds! "We've seen Him! He's risen!" they shouted, but were completely written off.

The disciples' reaction came not only from their difficulty in imagining a resurrection, but was also typical of men's chauvinistic attitude toward women in the Jewish culture of that day. Women were less than second-class citizens whose opinions mattered little. "They were strictly segregated from the social and religious life of their communities as inferior and unteachable creatures."[23] One group of Pharisees was called "the bruised and bleeding Pharisees" be-cause they closed their eyes whenever they saw a woman and wound up smash-ing into walls. A rabbi brought great shame on himself if he spoke to a woman in public.[24] One of the prayers that has come down to us from rabbinical literature says, " 'Happy is he whose children are males, and woe to him whose children are females.' "[25]

Jesus demonstrated how much He hated those degrading traditions by the way He orchestrated events after His resurrection. Jewish women were not al-lowed to be witnesses in court.[26] Their testimony was thought to be untrustwor-thy and of no legal consequence. So Christ turned that prohibition on its fat head and honored these women and Mary Magdalene by making them the very first witnesses to the greatest event in history.

The fact is that after the death of Jesus, the Gospel of Mark has the women take center stage, fulfilling the role abdicated by the anxiety-ridden Twelve.[27] We can hardly imagine today what a bombshell Christ dropped on His small band of male followers by deliberately giving women the leading role in the Resurrection story. I like to think He had a large, knowing grin on His face as He watched those women race from the tomb toward the upper room. He sent a crystal-clear message to His followers then and to His church down through the ages regarding the extremely high value He places on fe-male believers.

Jesus no doubt also put Mary and the other women at the top of His appear-ance list because of the special openness of their hearts to receive spiritual in-sights and truth. Their humility and fearless dedication made them ideal candi-dates to carry the news of His resurrection to the cowering disciples and to an ever-widening circle of people yearning for hope.

Like the Olympic torch that travels from person to person in different coun-tries, the promise of a coming Messiah had been passed from one Bible writer to the next throughout the Old Testament. Now these faithful women were given the great honor of holding that same torch high over their heads and igniting the unquenchable, New Testament–gospel flame.

[1] Ellen G. White, *The Story of Jesus,* p. 157.

[2] Leon Morris, *The Gospel According to John,* p. 831.

[3] Ellen G. White, *Lift Him Up,* p. 99.

[4] Morris, pp. 837, 838.

[5] Morton Kelsey, *The Drama of the Resurrection,* p. 32.

[6] Morris, p. 839.

[7] Ellen G. White, *Spiritual Gifts,* 1:73.

[8] Kelsey, p. 33.

[9] Morris, p. 839.

[10] Morris, p. 840.

[11] Kelsey, p. 34.

[12] Siegfried Horn, *Seventh-day Adventist Bible Dictionary,* p. 690.

[13] Ibid., p. 945.

[14] *The Seventh-day Adventist Bible Commentary,* 5:657.

[15] *The New Interpreter's Bible* (Nashville: Abingdon Press, 1995), 9:175.

[16] *The Desire of Ages,* p. 788.

[17] Web site: www.ashmol.ox.ac.uk/gri/4sea1not.html.

[18] Web site: www.civilization.ca/membrs/civiliz/egypt/egtut01e.html.

[19] Web site: www.civilization.ca/membrs/civiliz/egypt/egtut01e.html.

[20] Web site: www.civilization.ca/membrs/civiliz/egypt/egtut01e.html.

[21] *The Desire of Ages,* p. 789; italics supplied.

[22] Norval Geldenhuys, *Commentary on the Gospel of Luke* (Grand Rapids, Mich.: Eerdmans, 1975), p. 626.

[23] Gilbert Bilezikian, *Beyond Sex Roles* (Grand Rapids, Mich.: Baker Book House, 1985), p. 81.

[24] William Barclay, *The Gospel of John* (Philadelphia: The Westminster Press, 1975), 1:151.

[25] Morris Venden, *How Jesus Treated People* (Nampa, Idaho: Pacific Press, 1986), p. 73.

[26] Philip Yancey, *The Jesus I Never Knew* (Grand Rapids, Mich.: Zondervan, 1995), p. 212.

[27] Norman Perrin, *The Resurrection According to Matthew, Mark, and Luke* (Philadelphia: Fortress Press, 1977), pp. 28, 29.

Chapter 6

Remarkable Restorations

A funeral service is being held for fifteen-year-old Len, the innocent victim of a tragic car crash. An overused tape recorder plays "When Peace Like a River" softly in the background. A wall of flowers and greenery surrounds the coffin.

The immediate family occupies four seats in the front row of the dingy funeral home. Sitting stoically, staring straight ahead, the father hasn't moved for ten minutes. Len's mother hangs her head and repeatedly wipes her eyes with a yellow handkerchief. A sister leans her head on the shoulder of the person next to her, weeping, while her brother chats animatedly with the people behind him, trying to keep grief at bay.

After signing the guest book, scores of classmates from Len's high school solemnly take their seats. A palpable feeling of anger hovers in the air at the unfairness of what has occurred.

The music stops abruptly and the minister enters, taking his place behind the plain oak lectern. After reading several psalms, he offers a brief prayer, asking God to give the family strength and peace. He then shares an overview of Len's life, emphasizing his scholastic accomplishments, his humility and helpfulness, and his wry sense of humor.

During the sermonette, most people stare blankly at the gray, metallic coffin. From a seated position, all that can be seen is the white silken material lining the underside of the lid.

Suddenly, the tips of four pale fingers appear from inside the coffin and curl up over the front edge of the metal. The onlookers let out an audible gasp. Women scream. There is a loud thump as someone faints and falls heavily onto the floor. Chairs tip over as people run from the room. The minister turns and stumbles back in terror. The immediate family is frozen in place, riveted, immobile.

Another hand rises from within the coffin and grasps the left metal edge, just under the lid. The fingers tighten their grip and strain. Well-groomed, thick brown hair appears. The right side of Len's face becomes visible along with the white collar of the Van Heusen shirt his mother had given the undertaker. More falling chairs, more screams. The accident victim pulls himself into a sitting position, staring straight ahead. He pauses to take a deep breath, then turns and looks directly at his family.

That story never happened, but it sends chills up and down my spine nonetheless.

Hang on to that scene in the funeral home and add a ten-thousand-voice angelic choir; glory as bright as a thousand floodlights; jagged lightning; ear-splitting thunder; and a major earthquake. You begin to get some idea of what the Roman soldiers experienced when they saw the Son of God emerge from the grave.

Those soldiers had a front-row seat and were paralyzed with fear. Later they stumbled out of the graveyard, wild-eyed and trembling, and became unwitting corroborators of Christ's resurrection. They grabbed people on the road and stammered, "Listen to me! Listen! I just saw . . ." and then their words would trail off into incoherent mumbling. Eventually they were able to tell the basic outline of the story with such earnestness that many believed.

Caiaphas personally interviewed the soldiers and credited their astonishing testimony enough to be utterly terrified. The saliva in his mouth dried up. He moved his lips but could not speak. Then, as the men-in-arms were about to leave, he managed to blurt out an offer to pay them big money to tell a ludicrous tale about the disciples stealing Jesus' body.[1]

Pilate heard the fearsome rumors too. He ordered the soldiers to be rounded up and eventually dragged the full truth out of them.[2] Unlike the faithless disciples, Pilate believed Christ had risen, believed it fully, and was beside himself with dread.[3] His chest tightened and ached as he thought about the possibility of coming face to face with the risen Christ.

The Roman procurator paced his sumptuous private chambers. Beads of sweat dotted his wrinkled brow. He couldn't keep his hands from shaking. "Guard, I need something for this miserable headache. Now! Get moving! Why do they assign me such fools?" he complained. As the guard scurried around a corner,

Pilate screamed after him, "Run, or I'll have you imprisoned for incompetence!" He gathered his robes around him and slumped onto a red velvet couch, breathing heavily.

He felt the only safety was to shut himself indoors.[4] Turning to his assistant, he ordered, "Cancel all my appointments. I'm not leaving. No one gets in here that I don't personally approve. I want this chamber sealed from all visitors. Put ten soldiers at every entrance, every window, every passageway. No one gets near me without written permission. Did you hear me? Written! You've been far too lax. That will end immediately. I need protection, you fool!"

As if the reports of the soldiers were not unnerving enough, Caiaphas, Annas, Pilate, the Scribes and Pharisees, the Sanhedrin, and the general populace in and around Jerusalem were in for yet another incredible development, an aftershock of major proportions. They were about to come face to face with some of the most amazing people ever to walk this earth.

When Jesus rose from the tomb, He wasn't the only One who came back from the dead. After vacating His own grave, the Son of God called many long-deceased corpses up from their resting places and restored them to life. Matthew records, "The tombs also were opened, and many bodies of the saints who had fallen asleep were raised, and coming out of the tombs after his resurrection they went into the holy city and appeared to many" (Matthew 27:52, 53).

The part these risen ones played in the gospel story is rarely explored, but it is in fact one of the most astounding events in the entire history of salvation.

We know several things about these resurrected ones:

1. *They were raised Sunday morning, but the earthquake at the time of Jesus' death had opened their graves the previous Friday.* Imagine how shocking it must have been Friday evening and all day Saturday to have numerous burial sites exposed to view as if a horde of bold grave robbers had struck.[5]

2. *There was a "multitude" of these resurrected ones.*[6] That means at least scores of people, perhaps hundreds, were restored to life. These Sunday-morning resurrections happened on an unheard-of scale. Dead people had been brought to life before in Old Testament times and during Jesus' ministry. But they were separate, one at a time, individual. On this remarkable day powerful supernatural forces were unleashed that resurrected a crowd of people all at the same time.

3. *They came from the time of Creation down to Jesus' day,* spanning a period of about four thousand years.[7] How they must have rejoiced to meet each other and realize that none of them could ever die again.

4. *They were martyrs,* people who had died for their faith in God.[8] Paul talks about them in the book of Hebrews. "Some were tortured, refusing to accept

release, that they might rise again to a better life.... They were stoned, they were sawn in two, they were killed with the sword" (Hebrews 11:35-37).

Perhaps this group of risen martyrs included two individuals Jesus mentioned during His ministry—Abel and Zechariah the son of Barachiah. (See Matthew 23:35.) Isaiah, Jeremiah, Naboth, and Gedaliah might have been among them. Jesus' own cousin, John the Baptist, could certainly have been there, with his head once again firmly attached to his body.

5. *These resurrected people testified in Judea and right in Jerusalem itself,* that the crucified Christ had risen from the dead, effectively demolishing the false testimony of the soldiers. "It was well known to the priests and rulers that certain persons who were dead had risen at the resurrection of Jesus. Authentic reports were brought to them of different ones who had seen and conversed with these resurrected ones."[9]

Those resurrected from Old Testament times must have initially been very disoriented, having come to life, in most cases, centuries after they died. In the unconscious sleep of death, they knew nothing about the passage of time. They would not have known the details of who Jesus was or the story of Calvary and the empty tomb. I assume that Christ and their guardian angels met with them on Sunday or shortly thereafter to bring them up to date so they could testify accurately. How their hearts must have thrilled to hear the gospel story for the first time and be given the privilege of sharing it with others!

6. *They came forth from the grave just as tall as when they died.*[10] Their risen bodies were the same height as when they were buried. Those who originally lived during the time period of Adam and Eve came out of the ground more than twice as tall as we are now, perhaps twelve or thirteen feet from head to toe.[11] That's as high as two professional basketball players with one standing on the shoulders of the other!

These benevolent giants from centuries past would instantly command people's awestruck attention. The Godhead could not have devised a better way to advertise the Resurrection. A multi-million-dollar New York ad agency could not have dreamed up a more spectacular plan.

Picture a Jewish leader from the Sanhedrin rounding a bend in the road and coming face to face with one of these towering individuals. The huge, resurrected man looks down and says, "Shalom. My name is Amariah, and I was resurrected today with Jesus Christ, the Messiah. Who are you?"

The Pharisee looks up. His mouth drops open. His hair stands on end. He soils his underwear. His feet seem stuck in cement. He stammers out a disjointed apology about Jesus' trials, beatings, and crucifixion. "I-I-I n-n-never th-th-thought it was a g-g-good idea." He drops to his knees and prays the most heartfelt prayer he has offered in years, quoting every deliverance psalm his mother ever taught him.

For forty days these risen ones moved in and out among the flabbergasted populace.

Appearances to Peter

In the afternoon of Resurrection Sunday, Jesus next appeared to grieving Peter. (See Luke 24:34; 1 Corinthians 15:5.)[12] Ever since his denials took place, the ardent disciple had shouldered a suffocating load of unresolved guilt and self-recrimination. He longed to see Jesus once again, if only for a minute, to pour out his heart. He ached with the knowledge that it could not be.

I imagine the Savior meeting the apostle while he was walking between the upper room and his home near the city. It was not unusual for a Galilean fisherman who did extensive trade in Judea to own a second home near Jerusalem. Extremely wary of the Jewish leaders, Peter made his way cautiously along one of the Roman roads leading north. After a while, the crowds thinned and he walked alone. The breeze felt good on his face, feeling like the stiff winds he knew so well on the Sea of Galilee. Yet the brightness of the day seemed so out of harmony with his sadness and perplexity.

What would become of him now? Would he return to fishing in Capernaum? Would he once again live only to pay bills and mend nets as if there had never been such a Man as Jesus? Would he simply go about his business as though thousands had never been fed with a few bread loaves and fish, as though demons had not been cast out of raging men, as though storms had not been shushed into stillness? Peter knew he was not the same man who had been content to carry on his father's trade. But now that his faithful Leader was gone, anything else seemed pointless.

Lost in his thoughts, he noticed a tall figure on the road up ahead about thirty yards away. The road was straight, and Peter didn't remember seeing the Man approach. The Stranger's robe appeared unusually white, and He was holding his arms out in front of Him as if ready to welcome someone. The image of Jesus beckoning Peter to come to Him on the sea flashed through his mind. Curious, the disciple walked on, squinting into the sunlight.

Suddenly Peter stopped in his tracks. The Person in front of him looked so much like Christ. The two figures were now no more than fifteen yards apart. Their eyes met for the first time since the denials. Peter had never seen that unique, compassionate look on the face of anyone but the Savior. It was impossible, and yet the disciple had the distinct feeling that he was looking directly at his Lord.

A familiar smile broke out on the Stranger's face. Jesus stepped closer and said, "Simon, it is Me. I've risen from the dead!"

Shock and amazement gripped the disciple. He clasped both hands onto his head. His bulky frame shivered with excitement, and his voice cracked as he yelled, "Master! Is it You, Lord?" Peter saw the scars on Jesus' wrists and the uneven row of puncture marks ringing His scalp, and he knew. He ran forward, fell at the Savior's feet, and cried out in mingled joy and repentance, "Jesus! I'm sorry. I'm so sorry. Forgive me!"

Christ knew that the fisherman with the big mouth also had a giant, loving heart. He bent down, took hold of Peter's shoulders, and lifted him up. He drew the big man to Himself and hugged him tightly for a long time. Great tears of wonder and relief welled up in Peter's eyes. Jesus released the disciple and walked beside him down the road with one arm around His follower's back. At some point, they sat together by the side of the roadway in the tall grass like old times. Uncharacteristically speechless, Peter simply listened as Christ reiterated His love, recounted the events of the day, and reminded him of His earlier predictions regarding His resurrection. After nearly an hour, the Son of God stood, looked intently at Peter, took a few steps backward, and disappeared.

Totally incredulous, the apostle scrambled to his feet and looked quickly around in every direction. He laughed boisterously then thought of the others who were cowering in Jerusalem and hurried toward the upper room. As Peter ran, he marveled at the kindness of Christ in appearing to him before the other disciples. Jesus had come to him not in spite of his denials, but because of them.

William Barclay comments, "Peter had wronged Jesus and then had wept his heart out; and the one desire of this amazing Jesus was to comfort him in the pain of his disloyalty. Love can go no further than to think more of the heartbreak of the man who wronged it than of the hurt that it itself has received."[13]

This Resurrection-day encounter was actually only half of Christ's plan for Peter's full restoration. Renewal happened in two stages. In order to see the second half of the story, we need to jump ahead two or three weeks to Jesus' meeting with Peter and six other disciples by the Sea of Galilee.

By the time Christ appeared at the lakeside, Peter had already seen Him on three different occasions since the Resurrection. He had already experienced Jesus' warm, personal acceptance. But Peter nonetheless believed that the denials had ended his role as a member of the Twelve. The other disciples themselves "thought he would not be allowed to take his former position among them."[14]

Now, when their little movement finally held such amazing promise and the Savior was again gathering His leadership team, Peter assumed, painfully, that he would not be among them. Being on Jesus' team was extremely important to

Simon, and the idea of forfeiting that privilege was a crushing blow. "Those terrible denials," he thought, "have cost me so much."

Clearly, Peter did not yet understand the endless depths of God's grace. Jesus had some wonderful news in mind for the burly fisherman. At the appearance in Galilee, He planned to fully restore him to his former position among the apostles.

The Lord's response to Peter is reminiscent of the experience of Roy Reigels during the Rose Bowl game on New Year's Day of 1929. At some point in the first half, Georgia Tech fumbled the football. Reigels, who played defense for the University of California, scooped it up and sped toward the end zone. Unfortunately, as the rest of his teammates looked on in horror, Roy headed toward the wrong end zone. It was one of the most horrendous mistakes anyone could remember. A fellow defenseman, Benny Lom, took off at full speed and barely managed to tackle Roy just a few feet from the California goal line.

California's offense took the field but couldn't advance the ball and was forced to punt. Sensing a golden opportunity, the Georgia Tech players charged at the kicker and blocked the punt in the end zone, giving them a two-point lead.

At half-time all the spectators and ball players wondered what coach Nibbs Price would do with Riegels whose unthinking error had cost his team so dearly. The University of California players sat silently in the locker room. Crestfallen, Roy Riegels sank to the floor in a corner away from the others, buried his face in his hands and cried uncontrollably. He knew he had forfeited his chance to play the rest of that critical game.

Nothing much was said until a referee entered and announced that there were only three minutes left until the second half. Coach Price looked around the room, then over at Riegels, and said, "Men, the same team that played the first half will start the second." All the players left except Roy. He didn't move.

The coach walked over, bent down and said, "Roy, didn't you hear me? I said, 'The same teams as the first half.' "

Riegels looked up with reddened eyes and replied, "Coach, I can't do it. I've ruined you, the university, and myself. I can't face that crowd again."

Price clasped the young man's shoulder and said, "Roy, get up and go on back; the game is only half over." Players from Georgia Tech later commented that they never saw anyone play as hard as Roy Riegels did in the remainder of that game.[15]

Jesus responded to Peter's failures in a very similar way. He made it clear that He still wanted His wayward follower on the apostolic team. Reinstatement to leadership would be accomplished through certain key steps that the Savior planned very carefully. Those steps unfolded on the shores of Galilee just as the disciples were returning from a fruitless night of fishing.

The first thing the resurrected Christ did was to miraculously fill their nets. His purpose was to take their minds back to the time when He worked the very same miracle at their initial call to discipleship more than two years before.[16] In this latest miracle, He was saying, "I called you back then, and I am renewing that call to you today, and just as it did then it includes Simon."

The second thing Christ did for Peter was to gather the seven disciples around a charcoal fire He had built on the beach. Of the various words the Gospel writers use for fire, only John utilizes the one pronounced *anthrakian,* and he does it twice. In the first use, he describes the fire in Caiaphas's courtyard the night of the denials. (See John 18:18.) The other describes this fire that Jesus built after His resurrection by the Sea of Galilee.[17] (See John 21:9.) By using the same word in both instances, John deliberately connects the two events. He is telling us that Jesus made the fire on the shore to intentionally recreate the scene at the home of the high priest.

Sitting near the Savior, Peter stared into the reddish-orange coals, and his mind was transported back to that fateful night when he sat around similar flames among Jesus' enemies. In the presence of the other disciples, Christ now asked Peter three times if he loved Him, once for each denial. Each time Peter earnestly affirmed his love, and Jesus responded, "Feed My flock," openly entrusting him with weighty responsibilities.

Leon Morris comments, "There can be little doubt but that the whole scene is meant to show us Peter as completely restored to his position of leadership. He has three times denied his Lord. Now he has three times affirmed his love for Him, and three times he has been commissioned to care for the flock. This must have had the effect on the others of a demonstration that, whatever had been the mistakes of the past, Jesus was restoring Peter to a place of trust."[18]

Mark wrote the earliest Gospel, and he tells about Peter's denials in all their wrenching detail. Mark was Peter's interpreter, and most of his Gospel is a record of the sermons he heard the apostle preach in town after town. Therefore, Mark's source for the story of the denials was none other than the apostle himself. All over Judea Peter told large crowds frankly and openly, "Look at the terrible thing I did, and look at how the Lord treated me! He sought me out. He came to me alone, individually, because He understood my need. And it's because of His relentless grace that I was also restored to a place among the Twelve."

The forgiveness and acceptance Peter experienced from the Son of God transformed his denials from a source of shame into a wellspring of hope and renewal. Reflecting on his experience, Peter later wrote with gladness, "By [God's] great mercy we have been born anew to a living hope through the resurrection of Jesus Christ from the dead" (1 Peter 1:3).

After Peter professed his loyalty around the seaside campfire, Jesus got up and motioned for His disciple to come with Him. He wanted to talk to Peter one-on-one just as He had on the day of the Resurrection. In the quietness of the early morning they walked along together. As the waves rhythmically rolled onto the beach and shore birds chatted nearby, two sets of footprints pressed into the moist Galilean sand. Jesus had some very personal news He wanted to share with Peter, and so with great sensitivity and consideration He took him for a stroll away from the others.

Such immense respect for individuals had always been characteristic of Jesus' ministry. One of the most memorable examples occurred when, about seven months earlier, He healed a man who could not hear or speak. (See Mark 7:33.) Anticipating that the man might be startled or confused by what He was about to do, Jesus led him away to a place where they could be alone. The Lord then used a type of homemade sign language to explain the procedure for healing. Christ put His fingers into the man's ears, indicating, "I'm going to heal your hearing." Knowing that the people of that day thought saliva had curative properties, Jesus spit on His hand and touched the man's tongue, indicating, "I'm also going to heal your speech." Finally, He looked up to heaven as if to say, "This healing will come from God." Each individual Jesus spoke to, whether bum or billionaire, had His full, tailor-made attention.

At the sea, Jesus treated Peter with the utmost thoughtfulness and understanding. As they walked along the shore, He told the apostle, " 'When you were young, you were able to do as you liked and go wherever you wanted to; but when you are old, you will stretch out your hands and others will direct you and take you where you don't want to go' " (John 21:18, TLB). Here were three vital pieces of information.

First, "Peter, you're going to grow old. You will not die prematurely. Through all your upcoming trials, you will not be cut down before you are an aged man."

Second, "You're going to remain faithful to Me until the end. You will never deny Me again as you did at the trials. Instead, you will be like a rock, as your name indicates."

And *third,* "You are going to be crucified, just like Me."[19]

Just as Jesus had previously warned the apostle of his upcoming denials, He now informed him of his future crucifixion so that when it happened he would know it was something seen far in advance by God. Heaven knew all about it and would sustain him every step of the way.[20]

These three revelations also taught Peter important truths about Christ's kingdom that he could later share with the others. If the apostle was to become a senior citizen, the coming kingdom could not be imminent. A future crucifixion meant that the Romans would not be overcome by force in Peter's lifetime, but they would instead appear to overcome him. And Jesus' call to endure torture made it clear that His kingdom was about submission and sacrifice, not power and prestige.

Peter placed the Savior's words deep within his heart and pondered them for years. Not long before his death he penned thoughts taken directly from the scene around that shoreline campfire more than thirty years before.[21] In 1 Peter 5:2 he wrote to the church elders, *"Feed the flock of God; care* for it willingly, not grudgingly; not for what you will get out of it but because you are eager to serve the Lord" (TLB, italics supplied).

And then in 2 Peter 1:14 he referred to Jesus' prediction of his death. "Knowing that shortly I must put off my tent, *just as our Lord Jesus Christ showed me"* (NKJV, italics supplied). At the time of his death, Peter demonstrated great humility and courage, asking his executioners to crucify him with his head downward, thinking it too great an honor to suffer in the same way as his Lord.[22]

------

[1] *The Desire of Ages,* pp. 781, 782.

[2] Ibid., p. 782.

[3] Ellen G. White, *The Story of Redemption* (Hagerstown, Md.: Review and Herald, 1947), p. 237.

[4] *The Desire of Ages,* p. 782.

[5] Ibid., p. 786.

[6] Ibid.

[7] *The Story of Redemption,* p. 233.

[8] *The Desire of Ages,* p. 786.

[9] Ellen G. White, *The Spirit of Prophecy* (1878), 3:223.

[10] Ellen G. White, *Spiritual Gifts* (1858), 1:69, 70. See also *Early Writings,* p. 184.

[11] Ellen G. White, "The Great Controversy Between Christ and His Angels, and Satan and His Angels," *The Signs of the Times,* 9 January 1879, par. 13. See also *Spiritual Gifts,* 3:83.

[12] *The Seventh-day Adventist Bible Commentary,* 5:884, 885.

[13] William Barclay, *The Letters to the Corinthians* (Philadelphia: The Westminster Press, 1975), p. 144.

[14] *The Desire of Ages,* p. 811.

[15] Josh McDowell, *See Yourself As God Sees You* (Wheaton, Ill.: Tyndale, 1999), pp. 130, 131.

[16] *The Desire of Ages,* pp. 810, 811.

[17] Morris, *The Gospel According to John,* p. 754.

[18] Ibid., p. 875.

[19] Ibid., p. 876.

[20] Ibid., p. 815.

[21] *The Seventh-day Adventist Bible Commentary,* 7:548, 593.

[22] *The Desire of Ages,* p. 816.

Chapter 7

Two Eye-opening Meals

Appearance to Emmaus disciples

Quiz time. Have you ever heard of Cataument? Would it help if I told you that "Mr. Chamberlain's Woodworking Shop" used to be located there?

How about Buzzards Bay? OK, if those don't register, try Pownal. Nothing yet? All of those towns have two things in common: (1) they're holes in the wall, and (2) at one time or another I called each one home. For you they probably mean nothing, but for me they represent memories that encompass my roots.

Here's a tougher challenge. Have you ever heard of KRK? No, I didn't forget the vowels. That's exactly how it's spelled. I wouldn't have known a single thing about that town if my wife, Ann, hadn't grown up there in what used to be Yugoslavia. KRK is a beautiful, twenty-mile-long island in the Adriatic Sea. Her family emigrated from there in the early 1960s, to New York City no less!

As interesting as these four villages are to our family, they'll never be widely known. The primary way tiny towns get widespread recognition is if some famous person focuses attention on them. That's what gave a place just down the road from me—Kennebunkport, Maine—prominence as the summer residence of President George Bush (the older one).

That same kind of mega-boost in notoriety happened to a town in the Middle East that was so small, archeologists aren't even sure where it was located. It was probably nothing more than a common, everyday village like Cataument or

Buzzards Bay or Pownal, just a place to refuel your donkey and pick up a copy of the Judean *Daily News*. But Jesus immortalized Emmaus after His resurrection by following two people home.

I used to ask myself, "Why would Jesus appear to these two lesser followers before most of the Twelve?" Then I realized that I should instead be asking, "Why not?" The order in which Christ appeared to people on Resurrection Sunday seems to have been determined in part by a type of spiritual triage. Like a doctor arriving at an accident scene, He helped the most hurting first. The Twelve may have had the greatest potential for leadership, but that doesn't mean they loved the Lord the most.

The fact that Jesus put two rank-and-file followers high on His priority list shows that there were many people who loved Him deeply who are either mentioned only briefly in Scripture or not at all. It also shows that God has no interest in our usual criteria for hero making. He values deeds according to the love that motivates them. Imagine, for instance, how surprised the widow who gave a coin worth one-eighth of a penny will be when she discovers that millions and millions of people in heaven know all about her obscure offering!

Sometime around 5:00 P.M. Sunday evening, Cleopas and a companion began their two-hour journey back home to Emmaus, about eight miles from Jerusalem. Calvary had decimated their hope that Jesus was the long-awaited Messiah who would overthrow the Romans. They had grieved in Jerusalem during Sabbath and remained in the upper room most of Sunday. Along with the other disciples, these men dismissed the news of a resurrection. Like spectators after a fire, they saw no point in hanging around any longer and chose to return home to their jobs.

Jesus caught up with them early in their journey but disguised His identity. The two men were weeping openly and debating the events of the last few days.[1] Christ overheard them talking about a crucified Messiah and asked, " 'You seem to be in a deep discussion about something. . . . What are you so concerned about?' " (Luke 24:17, TLB).

Incredulous, they replied, " 'Are you the only visitor to Jerusalem who does not know the things that have happened there in these days?' " (Luke 24:18). Put another way, "Have you been living on another planet lately?"

The conversation that ensued was, without question, one of the most ironic exchanges in Scripture as they attempted to inform the Son of God about His own arrest and crucifixion.

As an analogy, imagine someone named Fred sitting on a plane next to the window. The plane levels off at 30,000 feet, and he strikes up a conversation with the man seated next to him. The stranger notices a computer magazine in Fred's lap and inquires, "So, do you think computers are useful?"

Fred leans back with a look of astonishment and replies, "Are computers useful? Are you kidding? Where have you been for the last twenty years? Without computers our whole way of life would be drastically altered! I've owned two of them so I should know."

Fred then walks his seatmate through a basic overview of how the computer was developed. He takes out his own laptop, opens it reverently, and says, "Now you don't need to be afraid of these things at all. See how easy it is to turn on? Then you just move the arrow around the screen, point to what you want, and click. Neat, huh? These little pop-up messages will help if you get stuck. I'm sure you could get the hang of it after a while." The conversation is interrupted as the flight attendant brings a snack and drinks.

After a couple of hours, the plane lands and Fred gives the man his business card along with a generous offer. "If I can ever help you pick out a computer to buy, please don't hesitate to call."

As a courtesy, the stranger reaches into his wallet and offers his own card as well. It reads, "Bill Gates, Chairman and CEO of Microsoft." Fred suddenly recognizes his seatmate as the pioneer and internationally recognized guru of computer software, heading up the most powerful computer company in the world! As he heads toward the exit, Bill says, "Thanks for the tips," smiles, and waves goodbye. Fred slumps back into his seat, stunned. The irony of the encounter washes over him.

In an equally odd exchange, the two Emmaus disciples turned to Christ and gave Him a brief recap of recent events. Cleopas spoke up first. "After the arrest, Jesus was tried by our Jewish leaders and then judged by Herod and Pilate. The Roman governor sentenced Him to be crucified. Crucified! You should have been there to see the spectacle! They whipped and beat Him, then nailed Him to a cross. It broke our hearts. It would have made you sick to your stomach if you'd seen it. We felt certain He was the One who would deliver us from Rome. I can't believe you're ignorant of these things." They too would soon understand the immense irony of their words.

Still concealing His identity, Jesus at some point took over the conversation and began to teach them what the Scriptures really had to say regarding His ministry.

"And beginning with Moses and *all* the prophets, he interpreted to them in all the scriptures the things concerning himself" (Luke 24:27, emphasis added). Luke emphasizes that Jesus taught *all* that the Bible had to say because these disciples only focused on certain verses and wound up with a grossly distorted picture of the Messiah as a Rome-smashing, five-star general.

What an amazing privilege to be given a Bible study by God! Christ, of course, knew the Old Testament intimately. When He had discussed Scripture at age twelve with the greatest biblical scholars in Judaism, "all who heard him were amazed at his understanding and his answers" (Luke 2:47). On a return visit as an adult to the synagogue in Nazareth, He taught the people from Isaiah 58 and 61. Luke records, "All ... marveled at the words of grace that came forth from His mouth; and they said, Is not this Joseph's Son?" (Luke 4:22, Amplified). Now, on the road to Emmaus, Christ gave His companions an hour-and-a-half tour of Scripture completely from memory.

When the travelers finally reached Emmaus, Christ was invited to stay. At supper He took the bread and blessed it. There must have been something distinctive about the way the Savior always blessed food, because when the two disciples saw His mannerisms, they thought about Him right away. They had to know Him very well to instantly recognize such details. When they looked closer and saw the nail prints in His hands, both exclaimed at once, "It is the Lord Jesus! He has risen from the dead!"[2] The Emmaus disciples had experienced the fulfillment of Jesus' promise, " 'Where two or three are gathered together in my name, there am I in the midst of them' " (Matthew 18:20).

Then, suddenly, Christ vanished! One moment He was sitting two feet away, and then He was gone! The disciples were left staring at an empty chair. Try to imagine how you would feel if you were eating with a guest at your dinner table and he suddenly disappeared. To be honest, I'd be paralyzed with fear. I give the Emmaus disciples high marks for not letting their emotions incapacitate them.

Sudden disappearances were nothing new for the Son of God. He had also vanished several times before the Resurrection. On one occasion His neighbors in Nazareth tried to throw Him off a cliff. "Shouts and maledictions filled the air. Some were casting stones at Him, when suddenly He disappeared from among them." (See Luke 4:28-30.)[3] He also disappeared when the Jews tried to stone Him on two different occasions. (See John 8:58, 59 and 10:30-39.) In all those instances the heavenly angels made Him invisible and shielded Him from human eyes.[4]

After the Resurrection, however, Jesus' glorified body itself had the ability to appear and disappear at will without angelic assistance. Now you see Him, now you don't.

The risen Savior could also pass through thick walls and doors. (See John 20:19.) Physical barriers were meaningless. He moved about at will. If Jesus lived in the Washington D.C. area today, He could roam in and out of museums, bank vaults, top-secret military installations, and heavily guarded government buildings without ever using a single entrance or exit.

We know from physics that solid matter is mostly empty space. A huge sports stadium, for instance, could be slimmed down to the size of a pea if all the space between the atoms and molecules was taken out.[5] Perhaps those empty areas provided some wiggle room for Christ's new body to somehow slip through. Or He may have been able to move among other dimensions beyond the measly three we inhabit. We really have no idea how He did it. We'll have to wait to ask Him.

Christ appeared and disappeared in dramatic fashion to show that He now possessed a body that was no longer subject to the horrid physical limitations imposed on us by generations of evil. From the perspective of unfallen worlds, we clearly live an extremely constricted existence. We are like the eagle that thinks living in a tiny cage in the basement of an old battered house is normal. Jesus' vanishing act proves that it is not.

George Ladd observes that the Lord's risen body "possessed capacities never before experienced on earth…. The resurrected body of Jesus possessed new and amazing powers. It seemed to belong to a different order of reality."[6]

My aging body desperately needs to belong to a new order of reality. Something inside me fell down and is causing my stomach to pooch way out. Fistfuls of hair have started growing out of my ears and nostrils. My wife has to say everything to me twice. My scalp looks as though inconsiderate loggers did some clear-cutting. The people at the pharmacy know me by my first name and have memorized my prescriptions. Not good.

I yearn for the day Paul envisioned when he wrote, "The bodies we have now embarrass us, for they become sick and die; but they will be full of glory when we come back to life again. Yes, they are weak, dying bodies now, but when we live again they will be full of strength" (1 Corinthians 15:43, TLB). The apostle taught that the new bodies we are given after the resurrection will be like Christ's. (See Philippians 3:21.) I trust that, just like our Lord, we too will one day be able to vanish and pass through walls and doors as if they weren't even there.

Appearance to disciples in the upper room (without Thomas)

Ignoring the lateness of the hour and the dangers lurking in a moonless, pitch-black night, the Emmaus disciples immediately headed back to the upper room. Parts of the road were rugged and unsafe, forcing them to scramble over inclines and navigate between jagged rocks. They wandered off the path and groped to find it again, alternately running and walking, pressing forward as fast as possible. Unseen, Christ was close by their side the entire way.[7]

Sometime after 9:00 P.M., the two disciples hurried into Jerusalem, negotiated several side streets, then rushed up a stairway to the upper chamber.[8] They banged on the door but got no response. Those inside were on high alert for spies and Roman executioners. "It's Cleopas; let us in!" The door was slowly unlocked and unbolted. Someone opened it a crack and peered out. The Emmaus believers quickly slipped inside.

The scene within the upper room resembled the bedlam and excitement of a newsroom during a big, breaking story. Luke tells us, "The eleven disciples and the other followers of Jesus greeted [the two from Emmaus] with these words, 'The Lord has really risen! He appeared to Peter!'" (Luke 24:33, 34, TLB). The Emmaus disciples then shared their story, pausing periodically to catch their breath. Though they wouldn't admit it, many now realized that the women had been right after all.[9]

Suddenly Jesus appeared in the middle of the room. Everyone reacted with terror. People fell all over each other trying to retreat.

One day last year, a docile-looking stranger approached four teenagers who were walking along a city avenue, and said, "I'll show you some magic." They hesitated.

The man repeated his offer, then huddled them together on the cement sidewalk and said, "It's OK, just watch." He stepped about eight feet away, turned his back, placed both feet together, and levitated four inches off the ground. No possibility of ropes or gimmicks out there in the middle of downtown, far from any stage props.

He remained aloft for six seconds (an eternity for that type of thing) then slowly descended. The reaction of the teenagers was immediate and intense. Wide-eyed, hands over the mouths, they all screamed and ran. Clearly this was not magic in the normal sense. Very spooky. Frightening.

I watched this encounter on a pre-recorded, primetime special on TV. I didn't run (Where would I go in my own living room?) but was certainly startled. *The devil must be doing this,* I thought.

"You should've seen what this guy did," I told my wife. "It's got to be something supernatural." My own words unnerved me.

I decided to go to the Internet and do a search on the gravity-defier's name. A Web site came up that contained the word "exposed." Turns out that the levitation trick was decades old. Drawings showed how anyone could do it. Smoke and mirrors. I felt duped.

But Jesus was no magic act. He really did do remarkable supernatural things. Appearing out of thin air in the middle of the upper room qualifies, in my book, as a first-class, hair-raising event. It is perfectly understandable why the disciples thought, *This has got to be a spirit.* How else could He have entered? It is easy to see why they acted like those teenagers, recoiling and wanting to run.

Christ showed the disciples the scars on His hands, side, and feet, but they were unconvinced. Ever patient, He sat down and ate a meal. He told them, "Spirits don't eat solid food, do they? Give Me some of that broiled fish over there." They all stood around the table watching Him bite, chew, and swallow like spectators at a pie-eating contest.

The Gospel writers mention common, everyday Middle Eastern food at several Resurrection appearances to help us understand the reality of Jesus' new body. He is connected with fish or bread at the home of the Emmaus disciples and here in the upper room, and later when the Lord fixed breakfast on the shores of Galilee. Rising from the dead certainly didn't lessen Jesus' appetite. As the Savior finished off the fish and licked His fingers, everyone in the upper room finally believed. He was truly flesh and blood and not some ethereal, phantom, ghostlike person after all.

There was instant pandemonium. Several disciples gathered around Christ, reaching out to touch Him, cautiously at first, then with firmness. Others dropped to their knees and raised their hands to the heavens. One simply stared at the Savior, transfixed. Singing and prayers mingled from exultant voices. It was like fifty birthday parties and wedding celebrations all wrapped up into one.

After things eventually quieted down, the disciples must have been bursting with questions. "Why did You allow Yourself to be arrested?" "How were You able to come back to life?" "What will the authorities do to us now?" I'm sure Jesus listened carefully. He may then have said, "Look, I can deal with all these questions best by taking you back into the Old Testament scriptures."

The Son of God then gave the disciples a captivating Bible study that may have lasted two or three hours. It contained some of the same texts He used on the way to Emmaus. "He said to them, 'These are my words which I spoke to you, while I was still with you, that everything written about me in the law of Moses and the prophets and the psalms *must be fulfilled.'* Then he opened their minds to understand the scriptures" (Luke 24:44, 45, italics supplied).

I have often wondered what verses Jesus might have used. We can get a clue by examining which Old Testament scriptures the New Testament writers themselves employed as they wrote about Christ.

Matthew was present in the upper room and probably incorporated into his Gospel many of the same texts the Savior explained that night. In his written account, Matthew often shares an incident from Jesus' life and then tells us that it was the fulfillment of a certain Old Testament text. For instance, he describes Christ's triumphal entry then quotes from Isaiah 62:11 and Zechariah 9:9. "This took place *to fulfil what was spoken by the prophet,* saying, 'Tell the daughter of Zion, Behold, your king is coming to you, humble, and mounted on an ass, and on a colt, the foal of an ass' " (Matthew 21:4, 5, italics supplied).

John also may have used verses he heard Christ explain in the upper room. Drawing from Psalm 22:18, he writes, "So they said to one another, 'Let us not tear it, but cast lots for it to see whose it shall be.' *This was to fulfil the scripture,*

'They parted my garments among them, and for my clothing they cast lots' " (John 19:24, italics supplied). After telling us that the soldiers didn't break Jesus' legs, John quotes Exodus 12:46, saying, "For these things took place *that the scripture might be fulfilled,* 'Not a bone of him shall be broken' " (John 19:36, italics supplied).

Peter was in the upper room that night and utilized Jesus' Bible study in his preaching. In one sermon he says, "But what God foretold by the mouth of *all the prophets,* that his Christ should suffer, *he thus fulfilled"* (Acts 3:18, italics supplied). He calls upon Moses as a witness, quoting from Deuteronomy 18:15, 18: "For Moses truly said unto the fathers, A prophet shall the Lord your God raise up unto you of your brethren" (Acts 3:22, KJV). He concludes with the sweeping statement, "Yea, and *all the prophets from Samuel and those that follow after,* as many as have spoken, have likewise foretold of these days" (Acts 3:24, KJV, italics supplied).

Philip was also in the upper room. We read about him later sharing part of Jesus' Bible study with an Ethiopian eunuch who was struggling to understand Isaiah 53:7. "Then Philip opened his mouth, and *began* at the same scripture, and preached unto him Jesus" (Acts 8:35, KJV, italics supplied).

On that amazing Sunday night of the Resurrection, Christ must have quoted many other Old Testament verses concerning Himself, such as the following:

Genesis 3:15: " 'I will put enmity between you and the woman, and between your seed and her seed.' "

Daniel 9:25, 26: "Know therefore and understand, that from the going forth of the commandment to restore and to build Jerusalem unto the Messiah the Prince shall be seven weeks, and threescore and two weeks: ... And after threescore and two weeks shall Messiah be cut off, but not for himself" (KJV).

Isaiah 7:14: "Behold, a virgin shall conceive, and bear a son, and shall call his name Immanuel" (KJV).

Numbers 21:9: "And Moses made a serpent of brass, and put it upon a pole, and it came to pass, that if a serpent had bitten any man, when he beheld the serpent of brass, he lived" (KJV).

Isaiah 53:5: "But he was wounded for our transgressions, he was bruised for our iniquities: the chastisement of our peace was upon him; and with his stripes we are healed" (KJV). (See also Matthew 26:31, 67; 27:35, 36; John 15:24, 25; 19:32-36.)

During that Bible study, the Lord also opened their minds to the astonishing vision of carrying the gospel to " 'all nations' " (Luke 24:47). For men who had never traveled more than a hundred miles in any direction, that concept must have stretched their minds nearly to the breaking point. Christ would reiterate that vision in His second meeting in the upper room a week later (see Mark 16:15).

Jesus then answered their unspoken question—"How on earth can all this be accomplished?"—by breathing on them and saying, "Receive ye the Holy Ghost." He puckered His mouth and exhaled like someone blowing out fifty candles on a birthday cake. This was an acted parable to show that the Holy Spirit was identical with the life within Himself. (See John 20:22.)

The word John uses for "breathed" to describe that upper room experience appears only here in the entire New Testament. It is also used in Genesis 2:7 when God created Adam. "And the Lord God formed man of dust from the ground, and breathed into his nostrils the breath of life; and man became a living being." Ezekiel employs it to describe his vision of a valley of dead bones that miraculously came to life. " 'Thus says the Lord God: Come from the four winds, O breath, and breathe upon these slain, that they may live' " (Ezekiel 37:9).

In his commentary on the Gospel of John, Leon Morris observes, "It is not unlikely that both these [Old Testament] passages are in mind [in John], the coming of the Spirit bringing both a new creation and life from the dead."[10] In the upper room this twin imagery captures the inauguration of Christ's new church through the miraculous reception of the Holy Spirit.[11]

All too soon Jesus vanished again. That simple upstairs room, borrowed from Mark and his mother Mary, had been consecrated by many momentous events during Jesus' ministry. Now, as the disciples lingered, they couldn't help reflecting on the stark contrast between their anxious outlook on the night of the Last Supper and the wonder and optimism they all experienced now.

---

[1] *The Desire of Ages,* p. 796.

[2] Ibid., p. 800.

[3] Ibid., p. 240.

[4] *The Seventh-day Adventist Bible Commentary,* 5:732.

[5] Morton Kelsey, *Resurrection: Release From Oppression* (New York: Paulist Press, 1985), p. 102.

[6] George Eldon Ladd, *A Theology of the New Testament* (Grand Rapids, Mich.: Eerdmans, 1974), p. 325.

[7] *The Desire of Ages,* p. 801.

[8] *The Seventh-day Adventist Bible Commentary,* 5:884.

[9] Darrel L. Bock, *Luke* (Downers Grove, Ill.: InterVarsity Press, 1994), p. 386.

[10] Morris, *The Gospel According to John,* p. 846.

[11] Laurence Hull Stookey, *Baptism: Christ's Act in the Church* (Nashville: Abingdon, 1982), p. 106.

Chapter 8

Beyond Reasonable Doubt

Appearance to Thomas and the disciples in the upper room

The situation couldn't have been more nerve-racking. The Boston Red Sox and the New York Mets were locked in an extra-inning standoff during the sixth game of the 1986 World Series. With the score tied, the Mets were up to bat. Mookie Wilson stepped to the plate. There were already two outs, and Wilson quickly got behind in the count, notching two strikes.

Everyone tensed as the pitcher leaned forward to read the catcher's sign. Several Red Sox players nervously hit their fists into their gloves. Others repeatedly adjusted their caps or sunglasses. The pitcher reeled back and hurled a blistering fastball. With a crack of the bat, Wilson hit a slow grounder that headed directly toward Bill Buckner, the first-base man.

Buckner was a much-respected, all-star player with an impressive .292 career batting average. He had been scooping up grounders for seventeen seasons. His only eccentricity was the out-of-style, high-top shoes he insisted on wearing. He claimed they supported his weary ankles.

As Bill stared at the approaching ball, everything seemed to happen in slow motion. The crowd was shut out. All of his attention was focused on that all-important, white leather sphere. He squared his feet toward home as he had done hundreds, if not thousands, of times before. It was a routine play, really. No spectacular dive needed. No rolling in the dirt. No giant leap.

Bill bent down and opened his glove wide. Half a second later he didn't hear the familiar smack of the ball lodging in the well-worn cowhide at the end of his right arm. Instead, he heard the second-base man swear loudly.

In less than six seconds, Kevin Mitchell ran across home plate from third and the game was over. And Bill Buckner's hard-earned place in the hearts of the Boston fans was finished too. Somehow, someway, the ball had slipped under his glove, through his legs, and out into right field. His error cost the Red Sox the game and ultimately, in the eyes of many, the championship. The reaction to his failure was swift and unforgiving.

Bill immediately became the object of relentless ridicule and jokes. That fateful mistake came to define the rest of his career. Richard Lapchick commented in *Sporting News,* "The grounder definitely led to years of anguish for Buckner, who finally moved from the Boston area in 1993 when acquaintances of his children continued to torment them about the '86 series."[1]

In spite of Buckner's loyalty to the Red Sox and years of solid play, and in spite of his community service off the field, he became known ever after as the man who let a World Series baseball go right through his legs. The label was unfair, but it stuck.

Something similar has happened to Thomas, one of Jesus' twelve disciples. His name cannot be mentioned today without the word *doubting* coming immediately to mind. The label "Doubting Thomas" is unfair, but it has stuck. There is much more to this good man's story than is usually told.

We first hear from Thomas about two months before the Crucifixion while Christ ministered in Peraea. Jesus had just decided to return once again to the hate-filled city of Jerusalem. The disciples were stunned. They said, " 'Rabbi, lately the Jews sought to *stone You,* and are you going there again?' " (John 11:8, NKJV, italics supplied). "To go to Judaea at that time seemed to them—as indeed humanly speaking it was—the surest way to commit suicide."[2] The disciples wanted to protect Jesus, but they also wanted to avoid being pummeled with rocks themselves. The fact that John the Baptist had recently lost his head turned the prospect of death into far more than a theoretical possibility.[3]

The disciples' fear is understandable. The Jewish leaders in Jerusalem had already tried to stone Christ twice in the previous six months, once at the Feast of Tabernacles and again at the Feast of Dedication. What advice do you think the Secret Service would give to a U.S. president if he wanted to return to a city where he had already been shot at twice?

Thomas stepped forward, looked around at his cowering companions and declared, " 'Let us also go, that we may die with him' " (John 11:16). That is a courageous statement, to be sure. But it gets a lot more courageous when you realize how awful stoning could actually be. It was a gruesome way to die.

The Jewish *Mishnah* describes the procedure. "Four cubits from the stoning place the criminal is stripped. . . .The drop from the stoning place was twice the height of a man. One of the witnesses pushes the criminal from behind, so that he falls face downward. He is then turned over on his back. If he die from this fall, that is sufficient. If not, the second witness takes the stone and drops it on his heart. If this cause death that is sufficient; if not, he is stoned by all the congregation of Israel."[4]

Listen to the testimony of a nine-year-old girl from more modern times who was hit in the face with just one hard-thrown stone.

"My health seemed to be hopelessly impaired. For two years I could not breathe through my nose, and was able to attend school but little....

"My nervous system was prostrated, and my hand trembled so that I made but little progress in writing, and could get no farther than the simple copies in coarse hand. As I endeavored to bend my mind to my studies, the letters in the page would run together, great drops of perspiration would stand upon my brow, and a faintness and dizziness would seize me. I had a bad cough, and my whole system seemed debilitated."[5]

TIME magazine recently reported the tragic stoning of two fourteen-year-old boys, innocent victims of the Israeli-Palestinian conflict. "When the searchers rolled the rocks away, they didn't see faces but unrecognizable pulp."[6]

Commenting on Thomas's willingness to face the stones, William Barclay writes, "That is the highest form of courage. It does not mean not being afraid. If we are not afraid it is the easiest thing in the world to do a thing. Real courage means being perfectly aware of the worst that can happen, being sickeningly afraid of it, and yet doing the *right* thing. That was what Thomas was like that day."[7]

So, the first thing we learn about Thomas is that he was a brave man who was fiercely loyal to Christ. "Thomas looked death in the face and chose death with Jesus rather than life without Him."[8] He was also someone who was willing to follow his own convictions no matter what others around him thought or did.

The next time we hear from Thomas is in the upper room the night of Christ's betrayal. During supper Jesus told His disciples more than once that He was going away to a place where they could not follow. He then paused and asserted, " 'You know the way where I am going' " (John 14:4). Every single one of those men sat there scratching his head, thinking, *I don't have a clue what He's talking about.* But, like students in a classroom who don't want to look stupid, they were too embarrassed to ask.

It was Thomas who finally spoke up and confessed, " 'Lord, we do not know where you are going; how can we know the way?' " (John 14:5). He wouldn't pretend to understand Jesus' words when he really didn't. His fundamental honesty and openness stand out.[9]

Thomas is quoted again after Christ rose from the dead. He was not present when the Lord first appeared in the upper room on Sunday evening. Instead of gladly accepting the reports of Jesus' resurrection from others he said, "Except I shall see in his hands the print of the nails, ... and thrust my hand into his side, I will not believe" (John 20:25, KJV). Strong words. So what's going on here?

The week after the Resurrection was a very difficult one for Thomas. At times he longed for the Resurrection to be true. But he couldn't bring himself to accept the fact that the Man he was willing to die for would intentionally ignore him. Christ had appeared to every member of the inner circle on Sunday. He had even traveled all the way to backwater Emmaus to appear to two less prominent followers. And, most mind-boggling of all to Thomas, He had already appeared to several women. *How could I be left out?* he thought. *It doesn't make any sense.*

I can sympathize with him. If someone told me that my father had just come back from the dead and had appeared to all the other family members, and even some of our neighbors, I'd have an extremely hard time believing it, because I couldn't imagine him ignoring me. We were way too close for him to pass me by, especially for several days.

Thomas eventually entered a very dark period of discouragement, mingled with resentment and jealously.[10] It only made matters worse when Peter and some of the other disciples came to him with huge smiles on their faces and exclaimed, "You can't imagine what Jesus did for us last Sunday night. He said several times how much He loves us. Then He gave us an incredible, detailed Bible study about Himself starting way back in Genesis. After that He commissioned us to bring His message to the entire world. Then, He breathed on us the Holy Spirit. We've never felt so empowered. Too bad you missed it all. Really too bad."

I suspect Thomas had a melancholic personality, and if a melancholic is in an emotional pit it doesn't help for sanguines like Peter to peer down at them and say, "Cheer up, ol' boy. Just listen to the birds chirping out here. Look at the sun pouring through the clouds. What's the matter with you anyway?" That kind of jabber only makes matters worse. While the upbeat disciples were warbling, "Don't worry, be happy," Thomas was singing, "Nobody knows the trouble I've seen."

Thomas stared up from his miserable hole and resented their joy. He fell into the "slough of despond," and his attitude grew worse.[11] In the midst of stupendous spiritual happenings, his thoughts turned sour.

Sometimes, my wife and I have had big arguments on the way to church. During the worship service, everyone is singing upbeat hymns. The elders are offering prayers of praise. The pastor is preaching about abundant grace. And I'm sitting in the pew in a melancholy funk, thinking, *What right does my wife have to be so stubborn and inconsiderate! What's her problem? How could she say such a miserable thing? She knows I'm right but won't admit it! There's no way I'm giving in on this one! Absolutely no way!*

Likewise, in spite of the blessings all around him, Thomas's mind was preoccupied with his own pain and inner conflict. In the midst of this hurt and resentment he repeatedly insisted that he wouldn't believe unless he could actually put his hand on Jesus' wounds.[12]

For most of the week, he had absented himself from the other disciples. But by the second Sunday evening, he chose to look beyond his pain and join his companions in the upper room for supper. That was the last place where Christ had reportedly been seen.

Everyone gave Thomas a big hug, a slap on the back, and welcomed his return. Then, while Thomas was reclining at the table munching on fish and figs, Jesus suddenly appeared right in front of him. The Son of God turned the dinner into a surprise party for Thomas. Christ came to the upper room that night specifically to see him.

The hurting disciple didn't have to wave his hand from the back of the room and say, "Hey, Jesus, look, I'm here this time." When Christ entered the room He turned directly to Thomas, who stopped eating in mid-bite and looked up in wonder at the loving face of his Lord.

Forget the finger in the wounds; forget the conditions for belief; forget the resentment and all the hurt. Thomas dropped to his knees and cried out, "My Lord and my God!"

It is important to point out that he ascribed to Christ an extremely exalted title—"My God." That was a whole new way of referring to Jesus. No one had ever done that before.[13] He equated Him with the mighty Jehovah, the God of the Old Testament. This marked a tremendous surge of faith. "This was the first time any of the disciples had realized and declared Jesus' true identity. Thomas the doubter became the first true believer."[14] Like the moment the ugly duckling became a swan, this moment of Spirit-given insight should transform Thomas in our thinking from a notorious doubter to a champion of faith.

Thomas's extraordinary words of adoration, "My Lord and my God," didn't come to him in an instant. The Holy Spirit had been wooing him in that direction for days. The prophet Hosea wrote, "Therefore, behold, I will allure her, and bring her into the wilderness, and speak comfortably unto her" (Hosea 2:14, KJV). After the Resurrection, Jesus allowed Thomas to enter a spiritual wilderness where the Holy Spirit could impress the mind of His beloved follower. Christ didn't call Thomas into that inner wilderness as a punishment. He did it because He saw in the young disciple a special readiness to receive a much deeper spiritual understanding.

Several great men in Scripture entered wilderness territory, both literally and figuratively, and came out spiritually stronger as a result. Moses, John the Baptist, and Christ Himself come to mind.

For Thomas that week of anguish after the Resurrection was actually a period of tremendous personal growth. Through the disciple's pain and loneliness, the Spirit was able to plant the seeds of a new vision in his heart regarding Christ's true identity. And those powerful seeds burst forth in the upper room when Thomas joyfully shouted, "My Lord and My God."

Something similar happened to the apostle John decades later. He crossed over into wilderness territory when he was exiled to a prison colony on the remote island of Patmos. It was during that period of terrible hardship and aloneness that John received the amazing visions that resulted in the book of Revelation.

What convinced Thomas Sunday evening that Christ had risen and that He was indeed Jehovah was not primarily the nail prints in the Savior's hands. The thing that evoked his cry of supreme belief and worship was the fact that *Jesus could read his mind.*[15]

Thomas had previously declared to the other disciples that three specific things had to happen in order for him to believe. He had to (1) see the nail prints in Jesus' hands, (2) place his finger on the mark of the nails, and (3) place his hand in the Master's side. When Christ spoke to Thomas, He cited that very same list, point by point, inviting him to fulfill each one of his requirements: " 'Put your finger here, and see my hands; and put out your hand, and place it in my side' " (John 20:27).

Thomas knew that none of the other disciples had seen Christ all week and could not have informed Him of his conditions for belief. He quickly concluded, *Only God could see into my heart like that,* and bowed low in humble devotion. Thomas thought Jesus had abandoned him during the prior seven days, but the Lord's words reveal that He had been very close during the darkest hours and understood fully the cry of his aching heart. The disciple now knew by personal experience that "the moment of greatest discouragement is the time when divine help is nearest."[16]

After the celebration quieted down, Jesus uttered His famous mild rebuke to Thomas—" 'Have you believed because you have seen me? *Blessed are those who have not seen and yet believed'* " (John 20:29, italics supplied).

Jesus' words are particularly interesting because He criticized Thomas for doing the very same thing many others did. (See Mark 16:9-13.) Even though the Savior's admonition puts the spotlight squarely on Thomas, the other members of the Twelve weren't much better. It turns out that the disciples were all doubters, but we pick on Thomas because he was so vocal about it. The other disciples had all rejected the witness of the women.[17]

When Jesus admonished Thomas, He was actually holding him to a higher standard than His other followers, and the crucial question is, "Why?" Why did Christ single him out? Why did He talk to him about believing without seeing and yet say nothing like that to anyone else?

The best way to find answers to those important questions is to examine other occasions when Christ intentionally stayed away from His followers as He did with Thomas.

The clearest example is the time Jesus chose not to visit John the Baptist in prison. John's experience is remarkably parallel to that of Thomas in a number of important ways.

1. The period of aloneness gave both an opportunity to rethink the role of the Messiah and give up their expectation of a military conqueror.

2. Both went through a period of doubt.[18] John wondered if Jesus truly was the Messiah and sent Him the message, " ' "Are you the one who is to come, or are we to expect some other?" ' " (Matthew 11:3, NEB).

3. And, like He did with Thomas, Jesus gave John a gentle reproof. " ' "Happy is the man who does not find me a stumbling-block" ' " (Matthew 11:6, NEB).

Beyond these similarities, there is another aspect of John's experience in prison that helps explain what the Lord was trying to accomplish in and through Thomas.

Jesus stayed away from John primarily for his own spiritual growth, but He also wanted to teach a vital lesson to the entire church. The Son of God knew that His future followers would face a period of persecution so intense that it could derail their faith and destroy the church. Therefore, through John the Baptist's faith struggle in prison, He made the important point that His followers are never abandoned by God, even though it may seem that way.[19] He wanted John and the church to understand, "Even though you are left to languish in a dungeon, you are still on My heart. I am closer to you than you realize. Don't conclude that I have forgotten you. There is a purpose."

The very same thing happened with Thomas. Jesus stayed away to teach a vital spiritual lesson, primarily for His disciple, but also for the church. The Savior knew that Thomas would not be present in the upper room on the day of the Resurrection. The Lord also knew that if He didn't appear to him at that time, His hurting disciple would openly demand personal proof—"Unless I put my finger on the wounds." And Christ took that well-known demand and used it as a "teaching moment" for Thomas and for all of His followers down through the ages.

Jesus had to make very clear the point that it is critical for people to believe in Him without actually seeing Him. Thomas could have been spared much pain if he had accepted the Resurrection by faith. And unless the church at large learned to believe without seeing, it would die out after Christ returned to heaven and the current group of eyewitnesses passed off the scene.

Jesus was preparing His followers for the time after His ascension when new believers would have to commit their lives to Him by faith alone. Years later, Peter commended his readers for that very thing. "Though you have not seen [Christ], you love him; and even though you do not see him now, you believe in him and are filled with an inexpressible and glorious joy" (1 Peter 1:8, NIV).

Christ had also stayed away on purpose when He first heard that Lazarus was sick. He let Lazarus go through the difficult, lonely process of dying and allowed Mary and Martha to grieve deeply in order to teach a crucial lesson for them and the church. By waiting four days to raise Lazarus from the dead the Lord provided unassailable proof of His divine origin and power. He also provided the basis for His followers to believe in the feasibility of His own resurrection.

And we must remember in all these instances that intentionally staying away was much harder on Christ than it was on any of His followers. It was counter to everything within Him.

Someone might react by saying, "I don't like the idea of Jesus letting people endure hardship in order to teach truths to a larger audience." But sacrificing oneself for the greater good is, in fact, at the very heart of the gospel. That value may jar on our sensibilities because of our selfish natures. But Jesus Himself set the example by suffering for our sake. He took our sins upon Himself that we might be saved. Jesus didn't "use" Thomas, John the Baptist, and Lazarus in the sense of selfish manipulation. It was because He trusted them so fully that He gave them the high privilege of partnering with Him in the accomplishment of His goals.

The apostle Peter captured the proper perspective when he wrote, "Trials will make you partners with Christ in his suffering, and afterwards you will have the wonderful joy of sharing his glory in that coming day when it will be displayed" (1 Peter 4:13, TLB).

Some time later we find Thomas in close fellowship with six other disciples at the Sea of Galilee. And when five hundred people gathered on a hillside to await Christ's appearance, Thomas went around from group to group excitedly telling them all about his previous difficulties and his breakthrough understandings.

---

[1] Richard Lapchick, "Losing out on their time to shine," *Sporting News,* 7 March 1994, p. 8.

[2] William Barclay, *The Gospel of John,* 2:83.

[3] *The Desire of Ages,* p. 526.

[4] F. F. Bruce, *Commentary on the Book of Acts* (Grand Rapids, Mich.: Eerdmans, 1975), pp. 170, 171.

[5] *Life Sketches of Ellen G. White,* pp. 18, 19.

[6] Matt Rees, "The Terrible Tide of Blood," *TIME,* 21 May 2001, p. 6.

[7] Barclay, *The Gospel of John,* 2:88.

[8] Morris, *The Gospel According to John,* p. 545.

[9] Ibid., p. 640.

[10] *The Desire of Ages,* p. 806.

[11] John Bunyan, *The Pilgrim's Progress* (Ohio: Barbour, 1988), p. 21.

[12] *The Desire of Ages,* p. 807.

[13] *The Gospel According to John,* pp. 853, 854.

[14] Kelsey, *The Drama of the Resurrection,* p. 61.

[15] *The Desire of Ages,* p. 807.

[16] Ibid., p. 528.

[17] Ibid., p. 795.

[18] Ibid., p. 214.

[19] Ibid., p. 224.

Chapter 9

My Brother's Keeper

Appearance to 500 people in Galilee

It would be only a few days until they would see King Jesus face to face. The year was 1844, and the prophetic interpretation of the book of Daniel by some early "Adventists" convinced up to 200,000 people in North America that the second coming of Christ would occur on October 22.[1] "From Canada to Maryland, from the Atlantic to the Middle West, simultaneously and almost unanimously, the [message] spread until every city, village, and hamlet heard the news."[2]

Luther Boutelle observed, " 'With joy … all the ready ones anticipated the day.' "[3] The Boston *Post* reported, " 'The excitement is very great.' "[4]

By mid-October 1844, many individuals were so convinced that the Savior would appear and put an end to this world that they did away with many of their earthly goods. The chief hatter of Rochester, New York, invited passersby to take whatever hats or umbrellas they wanted from his shop without charge. A baker down the street gave his inventory away as well. Henry Bear visited each of the people who owed him money and forgave many of the loans completely.[5] Employees in various towns quit their jobs, farmers left potatoes in the fields to rot, hay was left uncut.[6] Excitement reached a fever pitch as the final countdown began.

Their understanding of the prophetic time period was correct but, tragically, their interpretation of what event would be ushered in was not. As the momentous day passed and Christ did not appear, the people felt overwhelming disappointment and grief.

Two thousands years before that historic October, another group of people also greatly anticipated the appearance of the Lord. Jesus told His disciples during His ministry that He would meet them in Galilee after His resurrection, giving them the exact day and hillside.[7](See Matthew 26:32; 28:16.) Now that He had risen, the angels reminded His followers twice about that vital upcoming appointment. (See Matthew 28:7.)

Word went out, "Come and meet the dead man. Jesus is no longer in the grave." The invitation raced throughout the countryside, whispered from person to person so as not to arouse the authorities. People were filled with tiptoe anticipation, just like those who expected to see Christ in 1844. They journeyed along meandering roads and wooded paths toward the designated rendezvous. By mid-morning the hill was covered with expectant seekers.

Jesus most likely selected a hill that was already familiar to His followers. It could have been the same heights from which He had given the Sermon on the Mount about a year and a half earlier.[8] (See Matthew 5.) The evening before He delivered that sermon, Jesus climbed up the mountain and spent the entire night there in prayer. On those slopes He then ordained the twelve disciples to the gospel ministry.

Later, descending to the fertile plain of Gennesaret, He healed the multitudes. So many people eventually pressed in that there was no place left near the shore. Jesus led the vast assemblage up the mountain, where He located a pleasant grassy area that was fairly level. It was there, overlooking the busy lake below, that the Son of God delivered His revolutionary inaugural address.

Because of that remarkable day of healing and teaching, the mountain became well known to people from Perea, Decapolis, Idumea, Judea, Tyre, Sidon, and many other towns throughout the region.[9] (See Luke 6:12-20.)

The hillside where the risen Christ planned to meet His followers could also have been near Bethsaida at the northern end of the lake, the old stomping grounds of Peter, Andrew, and Philip. Sometime in March of A.D. 30 the Savior had gone there, hoping He and His followers could get some much-needed rest, but the inescapable multitudes thronged around Him nonetheless. One evening, on a mountain slope near town, He performed the miracle of feeding 5,000 men plus women and children. (See John 6:1-13.) After dark He stood on those same heights and watched His disciples battle a fierce nighttime storm out on the lake. (See John 6:15-21.)

About two months later Jesus went up to another mountain in Galilee and fed 4,000 men, plus women and children, after teaching them for three days.

(See Matthew 15:29-38.) This mountain was farther south than the one on which He fed the 5,000, probably near Gergesa.[10] In the late summer of A.D. 30 Jesus was transfigured on yet another Galilean mountain, probably several miles west of the Sea of Galilee. (See Matthew 17:1-13.)

Whatever hillside Jesus chose for His meeting, we are told that about 500 ultimately gathered there awaiting the arrival of the risen Christ. (See 1 Corinthians 15:6.) That is actually a good-sized group, considering the Man they were coming to see had just been executed for treason. Identifying with Him could mean big trouble. Galilee was the territory of Herod Antipas, and no one could be entirely sure that the whole thing wasn't a trap set by the wily king. He was headquartered in Tiberias in the southwest corner of the lake where, in A.D. 67, the Romans executed 12,000 Jews, sent 6,000 to help build Nero's canal at Corinth, and sold 30,000 more as slaves.[11] Those were extremely dangerous times if you happened to get the rulers riled.

It is not hard to imagine what the view might have been like from the Galilean hillside Christ selected. One could see fields of barley and wheat in uneven rectangles. Gusts of wind swept over the tops of the thin stalks like a hand brushing across an animal's fur. A ribbon of blue-flowered flax, one-and-a-half-feet high, meandered between poppy and narcissus. The hill itself was ablaze with mountain tulip and yellow chrysanthemum.[12]

A variety of trees occupied a wide slope to the left, trailing off toward the horizon. They were a multicolored weave of almond, large-leafed fig, red-barked cedar, and evergreen fir. Willow shrubs grew randomly at their feet.[13] A flock of ravens resembling a string of black beads scudded across the cloudless sky. Sheep grazed in a field three hundred feet in from the shore.

 Donkeys and oxen were parked along the base of the hill. Children rolled down the grassy slopes, laughing and giggling. Swirls of smoke rose up from numerous open-air cooking fires. Several women were breast-feeding. Old men took off their sandals to rub tired feet. A couple of dozen adults slept with their heads on rolled-up blankets. The disciples mingled with knots of people recounting all that had transpired since Resurrection Sunday. Multitudes were engaged in animated conversation, gesturing vigorously.

Suddenly Jesus stood among them. He didn't stride down the road or emerge from the forest or make His way up the hillside. He simply appeared out of nowhere. *That* kind of startling entrance surely got everyone's attention!

During His ministry Christ often taught hillside multitudes for an entire day or more. He could very well have done the same on this occasion. In His sermon that day He said one thing in particular that sent minds reeling. " 'All authority in heaven and on earth has been given to me' " (Matthew 28:18). He had volun-tarily laid down His rulership from the time of His birth to the time of His death. But now He had picked up the scepter once again and become the Possessor of unlimited jurisdiction.

Every job description spells out the scope of a person's authority. A maid oversees all the cleaning equipment and supplies. A storeowner has authority to run his business at the corner of Fifth Avenue and Chauncey Street. But Jesus has authority over everything, everywhere, forever. Authority over all the homes, businesses, governments, nations, animals, oceans, planets, stars, black holes, super-novae, angels, and all other beings throughout the cosmos. In the ultimate sense of the word, He is truly "Lord." We can take great comfort in the fact that this enormously powerful Person is intensely in love with each of us.

Christ also gave the hillside 500 the same commission He had given His disciples—to bring the gospel to the whole world. (See Mark 16:15.) He reiter-ated that vision over and over again after the Resurrection.[14]

The apostle Paul, writing about twenty-seven years after this hillside ap-pearance, adds the interesting note that many of the 500 people who saw Christ were still living. He had probably met many of them and heard first-hand the story of that unforgettable day. (See 1 Corinthians 15:6.)

Appearance to Jesus' brother James

In June of 1880, nineteen-month-old Helen Keller lost both her sight and hearing from what was probably spinal meningitis. Illness plunged her into a double dungeon of darkness and silence. Overwhelmed with fear and frustration, Helen increasingly lashed out at the unknowable world around her. During the first seven years of childhood, she tyrannized the Keller household, throwing temper tan-trums, hitting and scratching people around her, and smashing fragile lamps and dishes during periods of rage. There were other times, however, when she clung to her mother's skirts all day, desperately seeking solace and affection.

Her parents despaired of finding any help for their tormented little girl. Then, early in March of 1887, a "miracle worker" came into Helen's life. Anne Sullivan, a recent graduate of Perkins Institute for the Blind, entered what would become a life-long relationship with Helen as her teacher and friend. A victim of extreme poverty and terrible hardship, Anne became, in many respects, Helen's salvation. She searched earnestly for ways to help the young girl, and through resolute patience and persistence she opened for her a whole new world of un-derstanding.

In one of their first encounters, Anne refused to allow Helen to eat off her new teacher's plate, as the undisciplined youngster had been allowed to do with family members and visitors for years. Helen reacted vehemently, but Anne refused to relent and eventually prevailed. The next battle was to stop Helen from eating with her hands. After these early struggles Anne commented, "The wild little creature of two weeks ago has been transformed into a gentle child."[15] She never allowed Helen to behave in an uncivilized way again.

The famous turning point came when Anne repeatedly held young Helen's hand under the water from the well pump while simultaneously spelling the word "water" into her palm using "finger language." Over and over she associated the word with the substance and finally, in a flash of life-changing insight, Helen realized that objects had names. Immediately she raced from object to object excitedly pointing, anxious to know what each one was called.

Anne went on to devise a variety of innovative teaching techniques that included finger spelling in complete sentences with nouns, adjectives, and verbs, plus frequent ventures out into nature to fully employ Helen's senses of touch, smell, and taste. She shared with her the classics of literature, including Shakespeare and the Greek philosophers and made frequent use of Scripture. Helen's journey of personal growth and learning led her, years later, to earn a bachelor's degree from Radcliffe College, graduating cum laude.[16]

Never forgetting her own early struggles, Helen Keller dedicated herself to developing resources for the blind and the deaf. By the end of her life she had lectured in thirty-five countries and visited with scores of celebrities and world leaders to gain support for her causes.

In a very real sense blindness and loss of hearing also entered Jesus' household as well, affecting His brothers in particular. Instead of physical handicaps, James, Joses, Simon, and Jude were afflicted with blindness of the soul and a chronic inability to hear spiritual truth. Like Anne Sullivan, Christ tried in every way possible to open their understanding. Time after time throughout His growing-up years in Nazareth and during His public ministry, the Son of God attempted to help them comprehend spiritual realities, but to no avail.

Christ's brothers were a royal pain in the neck. Throughout His childhood they pulled rank and treated Him like dirt. They sneered at His clear moral perception and condemned His unwavering adherence to truth. They accused Him of having a superiority complex and scolded Him for placing His own ideas above those of the priests. Day after day they filled the Lord's life with hardships, threats, cutting ridicule, and baseless accusations.[17] I'm sure that many nights the Boy Jesus cried Himself to sleep.

After Christ began His public ministry, His brothers were embarrassed to admit He was family and thought He was out of His mind for claiming divine authority. They were around the Savior for more years than anyone else in the

Gospel story and observed His kindness and love more consistently than His own disciples. And yet they adamantly refused to accept His claim to be the Son of God. "They often saw Him full of grief; but instead of comforting Him, their spirit and words only wounded His heart. His sensitive nature was tortured."[18] Because of His brothers, home became for Jesus one of His greatest sources of pain.

Sadly, these men chose to vastly undervalue God's Gift. Imagine a family living in a drought-stricken country suffering terribly from lack of food. A friend from overseas hears of their plight and sends seeds that arrive in a large package with a picture of a juicy, ripe tomato on the front. An accompanying letter instructs, "Place the contents of this package in the ground about a quarter-inch deep and water regularly." Instead of rejoicing at a future harvest, the family feels that they are being mocked. They react angrily, "We desperately need tomatoes like the one pictured here, but all we get are these hard little brown things. They don't look anything like tomatoes! Does he take us for fools?" And so they scatter the seeds on the stone walkway.

Isaiah predicted that Jesus would be treated in like manner when he wrote, "He hath no form nor comeliness; and when we shall see him, there is no beauty that we should desire him" (Isaiah 53:2, KJV).

Jesus' brothers depreciated a priceless treasure. It would be like playing marbles with the Hope Diamond or wrapping fish with the paintings of Rembrandt or Raphael.

Christ spoke from personal experience when He later taught, "A man's foes shall be they of his own household" (Matthew 10:36, KJV). I can't help thinking that Jesus had His own family in mind when He observed, "A prophet is not without honour, but in his own country, and among his own kin, and in his own house"; and "whosoever is angry with his brother without a cause shall be in danger of the judgment" (Mark 6:4, KJV; Matthew 5:22-24, KJV).

On one occasion "came Peter to him, and said, Lord, how oft shall my brother sin against me, and I forgive him? till seven times? Jesus saith unto him, I say not unto thee, Until seven times: but, Until seventy times seven" (Matthew 18:21, 22, KJV). Jesus must have forgiven His brothers that many times and more.

I do have to admit that if one of my siblings said, "I'm God," I'd probably reply, "Yeah, and I'm the angel Gabriel," then collapse onto the floor laughing.

But it is apples and oranges to compare my family situation with that of Jesus' brothers. My siblings weren't conceived by a virgin or serenaded by an angel choir at birth. Wise men never traveled hundreds of miles to give them royal gifts. They've never been the fulfillment of a myriad specific Old Testament prophecies. And later in life I didn't see my siblings perform mind-boggling miracles or watch as tens of thousands of people hang on their every word. Don't get me wrong, my siblings are terrific people, but there are enormous differences between them and Jesus.

After Jesus rose from the grave, His brothers completely rejected the reports of His resurrection. Perhaps out of sheer curiosity they nonetheless accepted the invitation to come to the hillside in Galilee where the disciples insisted their Brother would appear.

The Scriptures tell us that after Christ showed Himself and taught the 500 people gathered there, *some doubted*. (See Matthew 28:17.) They apparently doubted that the Man before them was the same Person who had been crucified.[19]

As amazing as that response may seem, it is somewhat understandable for those in the crowd who had never seen the Savior before.[20] But the really startling thing is that some of those doubters *were His very own brothers.*[21] When Christ appeared, they looked at Him, heard His teachings, and said, "Why on earth did we waste our time coming here? These people are all chasing a fairy tale. The whole thing is a hoax."

The reaction of Jesus' siblings seems incomprehensible to me, but such is the power of stubborn unbelief. Jesus Himself had predicted, "If they hear not Moses and the prophets, neither will they be persuaded, though one rose from the dead" (Luke 16:31, KJV).

From a human point of view it would be perfectly understandable if, after years of hurt and rejection from His brothers, Jesus wrote them off, saying, "Forget it, they're a lost cause." But such a reaction never occurred to the Savior. In fact just the opposite was true. The more they acted like the devil, the more He loved them.

When James, Joses, Simon, and Jude refused to believe on that Galilean hillside, Jesus' immediate response was, "What else can I do to reach them?" With tenacity far exceeding that of Anne Sullivan, He refused to give up.

"Someone has rightly labeled Christ the 'Hound of Heaven.' He is absolutely relentless in His pursuit of the lost. When everyone else has given up the search and returned to their warm homes and busy lives, God still roams the hills, walks the back roads, and scans the horizon, calling out the names of His beloved."[22]

So, another plan to win His family formed in Jesus' mind. He decided to appear to His brother James. (See 1 Corinthians 15:7.) He knew that James, being the oldest sibling, could be the key to reaching the others.[23]

After the meeting with the five hundred, James had become increasingly troubled by the words of the Man on the Galilean hillside. He couldn't seem to dismiss them as easily as he had expected. Initially he felt the heady arrogance of someone who, unlike the rest of the dim-witted audience, sees right through the magician's trick. But now he wondered if he had been so discerning after all. The mystery Preacher's voice replayed in his mind and began sounding uncomfortably familiar. There was a unique earnestness in that voice that he had witnessed in only one other Person. He remembered wondering how the disciples had made the scars of their "resurrected Jesus" seem so real.

The apostle Paul tells us, "After that, [Christ] was seen of James" (1 Corinthians 15:7). Perhaps, as James walked along a road toward Nazareth, he had the distinct feeling that he was being followed. It was like the feeling one gets in anticipation of a potential change in the weather—a slight coolness across the skin or an unexpected swirl of an afternoon breeze.

He glanced around, but only casually, not wanting to tip off any observer or look foolish if he was wrong. Seeing no one, he resumed his walk. The length of his own shadow reminded him of the lateness of the day, and he quickened his pace.

After five minutes, he again felt a presence nearby. He bent down, picked up a rock, then looked around again, this time more carefully.

He had barely resumed his journey when another long shadow appeared alongside his own. Alarmed, he spun around and stared directly into the eyes of a Man who looked too dignified to be a threat. James stepped back and studied the Man's features. Neither said anything for several uneasy moments. Then the Stranger spoke gently, "Wasn't My appearance at the hillside enough for you to believe?" The voice was unmistakable, the reference to Galilee startling. James involuntarily began to shiver. His Companion continued, "Don't be afraid, My brother. I have risen, just as I predicted."

In a flash of overdue insight, James believed. Frenzied feelings of astonishment, guilt, and joy overwhelmed him, as the incredible truth finally became clear. During the next two hours, Jesus shared from Scripture, gave James personal assurances of His love, and urged him to try and change the thinking of the rest of the brothers. Then, suddenly, He disappeared.

Incredible thoughts and reflections must have swirled through James's mind during the next several days. In that one encounter his world had been turned upside down, or, more accurately, right side up. His thinking had to dramatically expand from thinking of Jesus as simply a fellow Nazarene and family member to accepting Him as the God of the universe! "I grew up alongside my own Savior!" he marveled. "I shoved Yahweh into mud puddles!" Immediately he began to think how he could share this astonishing news with his brothers as Jesus had requested.

James must have soon found a way to convince the other siblings to believe. By the time the scene shifts to the upper room again, after the Ascension, we are told, "All these with one accord devoted themselves to prayer, together with the women and Mary the mother of Jesus, *and with his brothers"* (Acts 1:14, italics supplied). Christ's brothers believed and were all there!

The experience of Christ's family is similar in many respects to that of Joseph and his older brothers. Joseph was at first despised then became elevated to great power and saved his family from famine. Jesus followed a similar journey and saved His brothers from a famine of the soul.

The conversion of James was not unlike that of the apostle Paul in its drama and significance. Jesus' brother eventually became a prominent leader of the Christian church in Jerusalem. Paul calls him one of the three "pillars," along with Peter and John. (See Galatians 2:9.) His leadership abilities and widespread spiritual influence led to his being chosen to chair the critical meeting in A.D. 49, where it was decided that Gentile converts to Christianity would not be required to follow the traditions of the Jews.[24] (See Acts 15:13.)

In the minds of many, the most likely author of the New Testament book of James is none other than the Lord's brother.[25] Knowing this background, I now look at that weighty little book with new eyes. It is stirring to read what he later wrote about Christ. In the remarkable opening verse of his epistle he calls his younger Brother "Lord"—"James, a servant of God and of the *Lord* Jesus Christ" (James 1:1, KJV, emphasis supplied). He later describes Christ in wonderfully admiring terms. "When you realize your worthlessness before the Lord, *he will lift you up, encourage and help you"* (James 4:10, TLB, italics supplied). It is also interesting to read James's admonitions against criticizing those close to you. "Speak not evil one of another, brethren" (James 4:11, KJV).

Jude, another of Jesus' brothers who eventually believed, also writes in his epistle, "Jude, the *servant* of Jesus Christ, and brother of James" (Jude 1, KJV, emphasis supplied). He fully acknowledges who it was that sweated profusely in the carpenter shop and ate fish and bread at the family table. "To the only wise *God* our *Saviour,* be glory and majesty, dominion and power, both now and ever. Amen" (Jude 25, KJV, emphasis supplied).

---

[1] George R. Knight, *Millennial Fever* (Nampa, Idaho: Pacific Press, 1993), p. 213.
[2] C. Mervyn Maxwell, *Tell It to the World: The Story of Seventh-day Adventists* (Nampa, Idaho: Pacific Press, 1976), p.32.
[3] *Millennial Fever,* p. 214.
[4] Ibid., p. 216.

[5] Ibid., p. 209.

[6] *Tell It to the World,* p. 32.

[7] *The Desire of Ages,* p. 818.

[8] *The Seventh-day Adventist Bible Commentary,* 5:322.

[9] *The Desire of Ages,* p. 298.

[10] *The Seventh-day Adventist Bible Commentary,* 5:423, 424.

[11] David Noel Freedman, *The Anchor Bible Dictionary* (New York: Doubleday, 1992), 4:464.

[12] Pat Alexander, *The Lion Encyclopedia of the Bible* (Oxford, 1986), pp. 14, 15.

[13] Ibid., pp. 16, 17.

[14] *The Desire of Ages,* p. 818.

[15] Dorothy Herrmann, *Helen Keller: A Life* (New York: Alfred A. Knopf, 1998), p. 44.

[16] Ibid., pp. 137–139.

[17] *The Desire of Ages,* pp. 86–90.

[18] Ibid., p. 326.

[19] Morris, *The Gospel According to Matthew,* p. 745.

[20] *The Desire of Ages,* p. 819.

[21] *The Seventh-day Adventist Bible Commentary,* 6:1054.

[22] Kim Johnson, *Spiritual Body Building* (Ministerial Association of the General Conference of Seventh-day Adventists, 1997), p. 8.

[23] *Seventh-day Adventist Bible Dictionary,* pp. 548, 549.

[24] Ibid., p. 549.

[25] Everett F. Harrison, *Introduction to the New Testament*, (Grand Rapids, Mich.: Eerdmans, 1971), pp. 386, 387. See also *Seventh-day Adventist Bible Dictionary,* p. 549.

Chapter 10

Group Flight to Glory

The Ascension

After forty days of post-Resurrection appearances, it was time for Christ to leave this dangerous, ungrateful world. On His way to the Mount of Olives He and the eleven disciples passed through the city of Jerusalem. The stunned residents who saw them walk by were left scratching their heads and saying, "Isn't that the man the Romans crucified a few weeks ago?"

As Jesus led His band up the western slope of Olivet, He paused at Gethsemane to reflect. What memories must have surged through the Savior's mind—wrestling in prayer; hand-to-hand spiritual combat with the devil; almost dying in the Garden; Gabriel's rescue; the arrest; and the sustaining power of the Spirit. The disciples themselves surely winced as they gazed at the Garden gate and recalled their callous slumber at the crisis hour.

Christ then strode across the summit to the neighborhood of Bethany and motioned the disciples to gather close around Him. He so desperately wanted the best for them. Tears glistened in Jesus' eyes as He looked at each one.

In her book *Truly the Community,* Marva Dawn recounts a time when her grandparents came a long distance to visit. She writes,

> One time as I hugged Grandma and said, "I'm so glad you're here," she laughingly responded, "I know; you keep telling me."

I answered, "I want you to know that forever. When . . . I can't hug you physically, I want you to find happiness in remembering all the times I hugged you and how much I love you."[1]

That same longing must have beat fiercely within the heart of Jesus as He anticipated leaving His intimate earthly friends.

The Savior rejoiced that He could provide the enormous resource of the Holy Spirit after His departure. But at the same time He must have experienced tremendous sorrow at having to say Goodbye. He wasn't like the released prisoner who smiles back at his cellmates and says, "Good luck, suckers, I'm outta here." Only He knew that the separation would be for hundreds of years. Only He knew the horrors His followers would face in the centuries ahead. That is why the Scriptures teach that once we actually get to heaven we will "follow the Lamb withersoever He goeth" (Rev 14:4, KJV). Christ doesn't want the necessary separation that occurred at the Ascension to ever be repeated.

It was at this point on Olivet that the disciples asked what has got to be one of the top-five worst questions ever. They inquired, " 'Lord, will you at this time restore the kingdom to Israel?' " (Acts 1:6). In other words, "Are You now, finally, going to demolish the Romans?"

Jesus was about to leave for a very long time, and that was certainly the last question He wanted to hear. During His three years of public ministry and forty days of post-Resurrection appearances, the Lord tried to tell these men that the answer to that distressingly persistent question was a huge *"No!"* "I am *not* going to battle the Romans, ever! I am *not* going to throw Pilate off his illegitimate throne." Jesus' kingdom would conquer minds, not monarchies, and hearts, not heartlands.

Right up until the end, the apostles didn't get it. Every one of them flunked the final exam on Olivet. But Jesus also knew that with the outpouring of the Holy Spirit coming in ten days, the seeds He had sown would sprout in wonderful, world-changing ways, and the true nature of His kingdom would then become clear.

Jesus' followers had no idea that these would be their last moments with the Master. They may have sensed that something unusual was about to happen, but nothing could have in any way prepared them for what their eyes beheld next. "With hands outstretched in blessing, . . . *He slowly ascended from among them.*"[2] The disciples let out an audible gasp. They knew He could walk on water. They understood He could overcome death. But to see Him float upward into the clouds must have been astonishing. (See Mark 16:19; Luke 24:50-51.)

Unlike many paintings depicting this scene, Christ did not ascend alone. All those who had been resurrected Sunday morning ascended with Him.[3] Gravity became a mere option, and they rose higher and higher like a flock of white-plumed birds.

Their escape from this world is reminiscent of an inspiring story from Colditz prison during World War II. Located in a castle near the city of Leipzig, Colditz was one of the most escape-proof POW camps in Germany. Allied officers who had repeatedly tried to flee other prisons were brought there. It was the only camp that had more guards than prisoners.

On a winter day in December 1943, POW Bill Goldfinch noticed that the snowflakes outside his window were drifting upward. That updraft gave birth to the seemingly outrageous idea of building a glider as a mode of escape. He soon convinced his best friend and fellow engineer, Jack Best, to join his scheme, along with Tony Rolt and several others. Ironically, a textbook in the prison library gave them all the specifications they needed. They began constructing the glider in their rooms, but then had to shift operations to the castle attic. Using shutters and mud made from attic dust, they constructed a false wall to hide their secret workshop.

Over a period of many months, they scavenged odds and ends to use as building materials. Nails became drills, and window frames were transformed into saw blades. For the wings they had to make six thousand separate parts. Floorboards and bed slats were used for framing. Sheets and bed bags, stretched tight and swabbed with boiled millet from scores of breakfasts, formed the wing covering. They had only one obsession, to escape from prison.

Their flight to freedom was slated for the spring of 1945. They were supposed to launch the glider from the castle roof and soar out over the German countryside, giving the occupants a healthy head start over the guards. However, as the launch date neared, the prisoners heard the rumble of approaching Allied guns and decided to postpone their daring flight. Soon British troopers took over the camp and liberated its occupants.[4]

The famous glider was never used. Its story nonetheless remains a testament to the intense longing of the human heart to be released from enemy bonds. Down through the centuries that very same yearning has burned within the hearts of millions who have cried out to be freed from a far more suffocating prison than Colditz, *the prison house of sin.*

On a certain day in A.D. 31, a multitude of earthbound spiritual prisoners were released by the Son of God, who led the most dramatic escape in human history. Clothed with immortality, a large number of redeemed sinners took their own flight to freedom, soaring from Olivet high into the heavens.

In one of his most memorable speeches, former President Ronald Reagan paraphrased a sonnet written by John Gillespie Magee, an airman killed in World War II. Reagan employed a phrase that seems so apt when applied to the resurrected ones who ascended into the heavens with our Lord—they " 'slipped the surly bonds of earth to touch the face of God.' "[5]

We get so used to saying the word *ascension* that we can forget what an incredible miracle it actually was. In order for that group flight to be successful, they had to overcome some very serious problems.

First, human beings don't naturally fly. Picture me standing out on an airport runway wearing a helmet and flight suit. The tower says, "Johnson, you are cleared for takeoff." So what? I could run really fast and flap my arms up and down and hop periodically to try and get started, but I'm still going to be tethered to good ol' Mother Earth. And if it wasn't for the power of God, the resurrected believers would have faced the very same difficulty.

Second, the higher you go the more certain it is that you will die. Last week I flew on Southwest Airlines from New Hampshire to Baltimore. I say "flew," but you understand that I was sitting comfortably inside an actual climate-controlled airplane, sipping soda. I can't imagine stepping outside that plane at 33,000 feet without a parachute. But if I did I would be entering what meteorologists call the troposphere, where the temperature goes down to as low as 80 degrees *below* zero Fahrenheit.

Fifty miles above the earth, the temperature plummets further to around 225 degrees below zero. One hundred and eighty miles up the temperature reverses and climbs up to a sizzling 3,600 degrees *above* zero. When the resurrected ones entered that area they would normally have been toast.[6]

In outer space the air pressure is practically nonexistent, so their body fluids would boil and then freeze solid. There is no oxygen, so they would all be unconscious in less than fifteen seconds.[7] As if all that were not bad enough, there is a thick layer of approximately 100,000 asteroids (hard rocks) to negotiate between Mars and Jupiter.[8]

Finally, there are the incredible distances in space. It takes light, screaming along at 186,000 miles per *second,* billions of years to reach many of the known galaxies.

I mention all this to help us appreciate more fully what an amazing feat it was for God to enable human beings to fly all the way to distant heaven.

As the joyful retinue rose higher and higher, the disciples on the ground below were utterly transfixed. They shielded their eyes from the sun and strained to watch. Finally, they saw just a tiny speck that became enveloped in brilliant light. The words, "Lo, I am with you always," drifted out of the sky like morning rain while sublime music from a thousand-voice heavenly choir filled the air.

The two angels who had guarded the Son of God during His earthly life immediately appeared to the disciples, taking time to comfort those left behind. (See Acts 1:10, 11.) They said, in effect, "Never doubt for one minute that this very same Jesus, the One you love so fully, will come again to be with you forever."

How eagerly Moses, Enoch, and Elijah must have anticipated the arrival of Christ and these resurrected ones from earth. As far as we know, until that point those three great spiritual leaders had been the only members of the human family to live amidst the glories of heaven. By the time of the Ascension, they had already worked closely with the Trinity and associated with angels and unfallen worlds for many years. They now looked forward to associating once again with men and women from home.

Heaven shook with applause and shouts of praise when Christ and the redeemed ones arrived. They were given the equivalent of a ticker tape parade down Main Street. Angels and other beings from around the universe leaned out windows, waved white banners, and sang at the top of their lungs, "Worthy is the Lamb that was slain to receive power, and riches, and wisdom, and strength, and honour, and glory, and blessing" (Revelation 5:12, KJV).

Simultaneously, back on earth, the devil raged. He knew the empty tomb ensured his own destruction. Christ was Victor in the supreme battle that began on Friday and ended Sunday morning in the Garden.

I am reminded of the decisive battle of June 18, 1815, at Waterloo between the French under Napoleon and the British forces under the leadership of Wellington. The two armies faced each other 1,500 yards apart, with 100,000 infantrymen, 28,000 cavalrymen, and 13,000 gunners serving 400 cannon. "One man remembered the sound of the two armies preparing to fight [was like] the 'distant murmur of the waves of the sea, beating against some ironbound coast.' "[9]

During his lifetime, Napoleon had led two million Frenchmen, and another one million soldiers from other countries, into some sixty battles, with horrendous casualties. He shook the foundations of Europe. The titanic struggle at Waterloo would now determine his fate.[10]

Napoleon launched a series of ferocious attacks, but each was repulsed. The final assault came at 7:00 P.M. When the French drew near, the British officers ordered their soldiers to conceal themselves amongst the standing corn. At the signal, Wellington's guns roared and tore into the great blue column. He immediately ordered a charge, and the French broke in retreat. Three weeks later Napoleon surrendered.

I can imagine Napoleon sometime later recounting that humiliating defeat. He walks up to a globe, runs his finger over it until he comes to Waterloo, and laments, "If it had not been for that place, I would have conquered the world."

In a very real sense we can see the devil today looking over a world map and placing his finger on the location of Christ's empty tomb near ancient Jerusalem. Like Napoleon, he cries out in bitterness, "There, if it had not been for that place, if it had not been for that awful place, earth would have been mine."

Appearance to the apostle Paul

I would be badly remiss if I didn't include another vital post-Resurrection appearance recorded in Scripture. Imagine the following scene. You go to bed at around 10:30 in your two-story suburban home. Your wife lies next to you, and the three kids, ages eight, ten, and fourteen are asleep down the hall. Unable to shake a strange uneasiness, you lie awake listening to the wind whistle past an open window.

Suddenly bright light plays off the trees. You get up, peer out the window, and see three cars pull into the driveway. You can barely make out several shadowy human silhouettes. Moments later there is insistent banging on the front door.

Alarmed and frightened, you grab your bathrobe, flip on the hallway light, and rush downstairs just in time to see the door being kicked open. About a dozen men enter dressed in ordinary clothes, brandishing rifles and semi-automatic machine guns. Three of them grab you, wrench your arms behind your back, and tie your wrists.

"What's this all about?" you yell. "Who are you?" The leader motions six men up to the second floor. Moments later they return dragging your handcuffed wife. You both are ordered outside into a van.

"What about the kids?" you yell as the captors shove you forward. "What's going to happen to our children?" There is no reply. Your wife screams hysterically. As you glance back you can see a look of bewilderment and terror in the teenager's eyes. Your youngest son is sobbing and crying out, "Dad . . . Dad!"

After a forty-minute ride, you are separated from your wife and deposited in a holding cell with nine others. You recognize them as fellow Christians. Every prisoner senses that a terrible persecution has begun. That evening more believers are arrested and crammed into a neighboring cell. In the morning four prisoners are given a mock trial and told that they must either recant or be killed. Later that day two of them are escorted to a backyard area and shot. Rumors are rampant that women are being executed as well.

That fictional scenario is essentially what hundreds of early Christians suffered at the hands of Paul. Luke tells us in Acts 8:3, "Saul was ravaging the church, and entering house after house, he dragged off men and women and committed them to prison." The word *ravaged* could also be translated " 'to devastate' " and " 'to ruin.' "[11]

In one of his sermons, Paul recounts, "I persecuted this way unto the death, binding and delivering into prisons both men and women" (Acts 22:4, KJV). And again, "I punished them oft in every synagogue, and *compelled them to blaspheme;* and being exceedingly mad against them, I persecuted them even unto strange cities" (Acts 26:11, KJV, italics supplied).

In Galatians, Paul describes his rabid obsession. "For you have heard of my former life in Judaism, how I persecuted the church of God *violently* and tried to *destroy it"* (Galatians 1:13, emphasis supplied). In his commentary on Galatians, Donald Guthrie explains the word *destroy* in this verse: "The Greek phrase (*kath huperbolen*) means literally 'beyond measure, excessively', and calls attention to the tremendous enthusiasm with which Paul pursued his persecuting purpose. Perhaps as he looks back he can see that even for a pious Jew he had gone much too far."[12]

TIME magazine recently reported the grisly story of a thirty-three-year-old woman who was terribly mauled by two large Presa Canario dogs in the hallway of her own apartment building. She later died on the way to the hospital. Her wounds were so shocking that the policemen who found her needed trauma counseling.[13] The early church viewed Paul like those dogs.

Five or six years after the Resurrection, on a road leading into Damascus, the killer came face to face with the risen Lord. A flash of dazzling light, brighter than the sun, caused Paul and his companions to tumble off their horses. They all cowered on the ground before the dramatic, supernatural presence of Christ. "In the glorious Being who stood before him he saw the Crucified One. Upon the soul of the stricken Jew the image of the Saviour's countenance was imprinted forever."[14]

Paul came to the shattering realization that in persecuting Christians he had been persecuting Christ Himself.[15] He understood that his persecution of the church was "nothing less than blasphemy: the sin he hated most: the sin he judged worthy of death. *He* is the blasphemer. Small wonder that in later life he should describe himself as chief of sinners."[16] At that pivotal moment in history, Paul began the journey from being the scourge of Christianity to becoming its greatest champion.

Years later, after cataloguing Jesus' resurrection appearances, Paul speaks of His own fateful encounter with the risen Lord. "Last of all, as to one untimely born, he appeared also to me" (1 Corinthians 15:8). And again, "I am an apostle. . . . I am one who has actually seen Jesus our Lord with my own eyes" (1 Corinthians 9:1, TLB).

Even though Christ called him to leadership, Paul assumed a position of great humility because of his infamous past. The apostle wrote, "I don't deserve to be included in that inner circle, as you well know, having spent all those early years trying my best to stamp God's church right out of existence. But because God was so gracious, so very generous, here I am" (1 Corinthians 15:8-10, *The Message*).

During the years following his conversion Paul tried hard not to dwell on his life as a devastating persecutor. It was far too painful. (See Philippians 3:13.) Nonetheless he must have often awakened in the middle of the night bathed in a cold sweat, trembling from a nightmare in which he saw again the pleading faces of those he harmed so terribly.

We can measure the terror of the persecution Paul inflicted by the difficulty early Christians had in accepting the genuineness of his conversion. When Ananias was asked to heal Paul's blindness, he protested that this was an extremely dangerous man. In effect Ananias said, "Lord, isn't there anyone else You can send instead of me?" Even three years after Paul's conversion, when he visited Jerusalem for the first time to see Peter and James, the Scriptures record, "When he had come to Jerusalem he attempted to join the disciples; *and they were all afraid of him, for they did not believe that he was a disciple*" (Acts 9:26, italics supplied). How would you react if you saw Hitler walking into a Jewish synagogue wearing a Yarmulke and telling people he had come to worship the God of heaven?

I would love to have seen the look on the faces of the angels and unfallen beings when, at the height of Paul's persecutions, Jesus announced, "I've been looking throughout Judea and Galilee for an effective replacement for Judas who can represent the Trinity well." They watch as He points to an enraged, determined man riding into Damascus with an arrest warrant for Christians and says, "There he is. I've chosen Paul."

Is it any wonder that the center of Paul's message was Jesus' resurrection? He had seen the living Christ, experienced His amazing grace, and it had changed his life forever. As William Barclay states, "His witness is not of someone who has lived and died but of One who is gloriously present and alive for evermore."[17]

---

[1] Marva J. Dawn, *Truly the Community: Romans 12 and How to Be the Church* (Grand Rapids, Mich.: Eerdmans, 1992), p. 164.

[2] *The Desire of Ages,* pp. 830, 831, italics supplied.

[3] Ibid., p. 833.

[4] Internet Web sites: http://www.pbs.org/wgbh/nova/naziprison/colditz.html and http://www.colditz-4c.com/glider.htm.

[5] Internet Web site: http://www.time.com/time/reports/space/disaster1.html.

[6] *Planet Earth Atmosphere* (Time-Life Books, Alexandria, VA), p. 63.

[7] Internet Web site: http://www.howstuffworks.com.

[8] Internet Web site: http://windows.arc.nasa.gov/cgi-bin/tour_def/our_solar_system/asteroids.html.

[9] John J. Putnam, "Napoleon," *National Geographic,* February 1982, p. 180.

[10] Ibid.

[11] *The Seventh-day Adventist Bible Commentary,* 6:213.

[12] Donald Guthrie, *Galatians* (Greenwood, S.C.: Attic Press, 1969), p. 68.

[13] Chris Taylor, "Terror on a Leash," *TIME,* 12 February 2001, p. 63.

[14] Ellen G. White, *The Acts of the Apostles* (Nampa, Idaho: Pacific Press, 1911), p. 115.

[15] G. D. Yarnold, *Risen Indeed* (London: Oxford University Press, 1959), p. 98.

[16] Ibid., p. 99.

[17] William Barclay, *The Acts of the Apostles* (Philadelphia: Westminster Press, 1976), p. 177.

Chapter 11

God of the Dead Places

"Engines eighty-two and thirty-one, get out." The insistent order echoed throughout the firehouse. Dennis Smith leaped onto the back of the pumper just before it pulled out into traffic, siren blaring. On 165th Street the fifth floor of an old apartment building was enveloped in flames. Smith donned an oxygen mask and headed up the front stairway toward the upper-level inferno.

When he arrived at the fifth story, he saw another fireman crawl into one of the side rooms and drag out the unconscious forms of a mother and child just before the room filled with fire.

Smith took the hose nozzle to attack the roaring flames. Crouching low, he moved slowly down the hallway amidst the clutter of debris, spraying the high-pressure stream of water back and forth. Suddenly part of the floor gave way, and his leg was pinned between two smoldering floorboards. "Easy now," he shouted to a fellow fireman who helped free him. Smith was immediately ordered out of the building.

Before exiting, he limped to an open window, ripped off his oxygen mask, and took in deep drafts of clean air. Suddenly someone from Ladder 31 yelled, "I gotta baby here!" It was a little girl who could have been saved if the alarm had only been turned in minutes earlier. Smith's mouth filled with coffee and veal as his stomach emptied.

Minutes later, sitting on an outside step, he looked up into the face of a fireman who held the dead baby's limp body wrapped in a borrowed bedspread. The man's reddened eyes were filled with tears. Smith reflected, "I wish my wife, my mother, everyone who has ever asked me why I do what I do, could see the humanity, the sympathy, the sadness of these eyes, because in them is the reason I continue to be a firefighter."[1]

Firefighters fight fires and assist victims. That is their job description. When everyone else is running out of a burning building, they run in. That is what they want to do, what they have committed themselves to doing.

Likewise, when someone is deathly ill, a physician will race to the person's side to provide assistance. That is what doctors specialize in doing.

Jesus Christ has a specialty, too, that fits His character perfectly—He is the Resurrector. And as such, He specializes in dead things. That is what He loves to do, what He has committed Himself to doing. The words *resurrector* and *death* belong together just like the words *firefighter* and *fire,* like the words *physician* and *illness.* By claiming the power to resurrect, Jesus revealed Himself to be *the God of the dead places.* The apostle Paul captured this theme when he wrote, "For to this end Christ died and lived again, that he might be Lord both of the dead and of the living" (Romans 14:9).

Jesus' resurrection power could give life to a corpse or to paralyzed limbs. But His greatest challenge by far was resurrecting dead hearts and minds. Thousands of people who looked outwardly healthy were dying spiritually, mentally, or emotionally, and Christ felt an overwhelming desire to help.

The following three accounts from Jesus' ministry all involve the language and theme of death in some way. In each case Christ as Resurrector was intensely drawn toward people who were inwardly dying.

After stilling the storm on the Sea of Galilee, Jesus and His disciples landed on the western shore near the town of Gergesa. Immediately, two naked men raced down from the hills, screaming threats. (See Matthew 8:28-34; Mark 5:1-20.) They looked more like animals than human beings. Long, matted strands of hair draped down below their shoulders. Broken chains from handcuffs and leg irons clanked and rattled on the ground. The Lord had chosen to put ashore at this very spot to get close to these needy men. Even at sea the Resurrector could detect the smell of inner death and hurried toward it.

The beastlike, raging duo actually lived inside a limestone tomb and had mutilated their bodies as if committing slow suicide. These were simply the outward signs of the many inner deaths they had already experienced. Death to family life and social interaction. Death to jobs and career. Death to dignity and selfhood. Death to purpose and meaning.

The disciples all fled, scrambling down the beach in abject terror. Jesus, however, stood His ground. He delivered the demon-possessed men, put His arms around them, taught them the gospel, and sent them out as the very first missionaries to the many towns and villages in the region of Decapolis.

When Christ returned eight months later, thousands were ready to receive Him because of the humble, enthusiastic witness of these two men. All this goodness happened because the Resurrector had been inexorably drawn to the stinkiest place in all Gergesa.

The second incident dealing with inner death involves the scribes and Pharisees. No group within Judaism was, in general, more spiritually lifeless. They vehemently opposed the Savior throughout His ministry, and yet there was no segment of society He tried harder to reach. As Resurrector, His heart burned with an overwhelming desire to give them life. He ate with these religious leaders and repeatedly taught in their midst, but had only very limited success.

While teaching in the temple on the Tuesday before the Crucifixion, Jesus told the scribes and Pharisees very pointedly that they were inwardly dead. He announced, " 'Woe to you, . . . hypocrites! for you are like whitewashed tombs, which outwardly appear beautiful, but within they are full of dead men's bones and all uncleanness. So you also outwardly appear righteous to men, but within you are full of hypocrisy and iniquity' " (Matthew 23:27, 28). Spiritual death lurked underneath their custom-fitted, sanctimonious robes.

Such scathing words can seem very much out of character for our Lord. Yet far from being the words of an offended God, they were the last desperate call of love. They were a last-ditch effort to get the Jewish leaders to understand their spiritual need.

If my daughter were playing safely in the backyard, I would talk to her in gentle tones. But if I saw her playing in the middle of a busy highway, it would be unloving to speak in a soft manner and say, "My little darling, you know Daddy isn't happy when you play in front of huge eighteen-wheel tractor trailers going 70 mph." The intensity of my love would be revealed by how loudly I yelled for her to get out of the road. Likewise, the intensity of Jesus' love for the Pharisees was revealed in the sharpness of His warnings and denunciations.

The third incident in which the Savior felt drawn toward death takes us to the Last Supper. John records that when Judas left the upper room for the final time "it was night" (John 13:30). John means much more than physical darkness. He is talking about the darkness of spiritual death within the heart of Christ's betrayer.

Ever since their first meeting, the Lord had tried earnestly to find a way into His wayward disciple's life. During their last hours together in the upper room, Christ reached out to Judas in several poignant and powerful ways. For instance, when Jesus took on the role of a Gentile slave and washed the disciples' feet, He washed the feet of Judas first.[2] Later, He allowed Judas to sit at the head of the table on His left, which was the place of highest honor after the host. He even gave Judas the "sop," a morsel of bread dipped in the drink, which in the Jewish culture of that day was a gesture of highest affection.[3] (See John 13:1-30.)

All during the Last Supper, Jesus drew very near to Judas physically. People reclined on their left elbow to eat, which put the Savior's head within inches of Judas's chest. He could hear the young man's racing heart, smell the sweaty palms, sense the nervous quiver of his hands. By His actions Christ was whispering to Judas, "I want to be very near to you tonight. Believe Me, My dear friend, when I say it's not too late, even now it's not too late, not really. You're leaning far out over the precipice, but you can still come back. Please throw away the silver coins. Please don't let them have you. Please don't go."

Over and over again during Christ's ministry the Author of life felt drawn toward inner death. The words, "Those who are well have no need of a physician, but those who are sick" captured the central, driving force behind all that He did.

At one point Jesus declared, "*I am* the Resurrection and the Life." He didn't say "I was" or "I will be" but "I am." There is a timeless quality to His role as Resurrector. He is ever present as the Life-Giver. As such, He longs to draw intimately close to the dead places within us today just as He drew near to inner death two thousand years ago.

By "dead places" I mean those parts of our lives where we feel defeated, helpless, numb, powerless, or broken. Those places that we often try to hide from others and even from ourselves. They may be the result of faulty genes, illness, upbringing, life circumstances, bad choices, or our sinful natures. No matter what the cause, Christ is always eager to meet us at the point of our deepest need. God's love flows toward hurt and failure just as oxygen flows toward a vacuum or water flows toward the lowest point of ground.

When I first went to work in the local church headquarters, two members of the treasury department and I had our desks on the first floor. It was a supply room in the basement to be exact, also known as "the dungeon." My desk faced the far wall. The two other desks faced each other with a support post wedged in between. The decor was "Early Awful." No windows, no carpet, no ceiling tiles, and lots of metal shelves chock full of various dust-laden, ancient items crucial to the future of God's work.

In November, some furry little shrew usually wandered into our work area trying to escape the oncoming cold. Inevitably it got delirious from lack of food and water, lapsed into a coma and died. No shrew ever expired where you could easily remove the carcass. It always chose to say Goodbye to this world inside the walls or in some other inaccessible spot.

Death smells, and within a few days the stench was enough to curl a person's nostrils. I would have relocated at the drop of a hat, but there was nowhere else to put our desks. So we did the next best thing and purchased a case of air-deodorizer. The unique blend of shrew fumes and "Spring Lilac" will be forever imprinted on my brain.

We all have dead places in our lives, rotten places that smell bad. We keep them under wraps, hoping no one will discover how deficient we really are and how seldom we have it all together. When an unpleasant odor leaks out, we quickly spray the area with the deodorizers of "I'm OK, you're OK," or "If you don't like that mask, I'll put on this one." We don't dare take off all our masks because people may not like what's underneath—and that's all we have.

Years ago, as a young pastor, I keenly felt the pressure to look holy. I wouldn't allow any church member within fifty miles of the smelly parts of my inner life. I wouldn't dare let any parishioner know that I didn't pray nearly as much as I advocated, that I hated certain obnoxious saints, that I was jealous of other pastors' successes, that I felt desperately unsure of my abilities as a leader, or that I struggled to sense God's love for me.

One day my wife came home from choir practice and said, "I finally let Mr. _____ have it. I really blasted him. I'm sick and tired of his sarcastic remarks."

I was horrified. "He's an elder!" I shouted back. "How could you do such a thing?"

I imagined him phoning the conference president then blasting me back at the next church board meeting. How could my wife be so honest and open right in church?

"You want me to lose my job?" I yelled.

My insecurities and fears were hanging out all over the place. Did this mean that the well-hidden smell of my inner neediness would be discovered? Would the whiff that church leaders got from my wife's words cause them to start sniffing around me like relentless religious bloodhounds?

As soon as I calmed down a little, I reached for the deodorizer. I made several phone calls to try and smooth things over. I catered to the offensive elder for the next three months. I tried desperately to manipulate my wife into acting like the sugar plum fairy from Tchaikovsky's *Nutcracker Suite*.

I wish I had understood back then how intensely Christ is drawn to the dead places in our lives, the smelly places I ran from for so long. Rather than being sources of embarrassment and insecurity, they could have been places where the Resurrector and I spent intimate time together, places that led to understanding, healing, and maturity in Him. I also could have realized that every church member struggles with inner dead places that stink just as terribly as mine do.

In the book *God Is for Real, Man,* a chaplain asked troubled teens from the slums to rewrite some of the psalms in terms that they could understand. One of the most poignant is based on Psalm 23 and reads in part,

> The Lord is like my Probation Officer, ...
> He tries to help me make it every day....
> He makes sure I have my food
> And that Mom fixes it.
> He helps her stay sober....
> I know the Lord
> Is with me like the Probation Officer.[4]

This young man lived in such an inner-city hell hole that the highest form of love he could imagine was a kindly authority figure from law enforcement. God's love shone upon him like the floodlights from a million baseball stadiums, but he could see only a tiny slit, a few meager rays. Our own God-concept usually isn't a whole lot better, even if we come from a home as ideal as the sitcoms of the 1950s. As sinners, our understanding of God is often terribly warped and distorted.

One of the worst distortions is that God draws back when we act like the devil, when our thoughts, attitudes, or actions stink like a putrefying corpse. That is one of Satan's most popular and effective lies. In fact, just the opposite is true. Jesus treats sin very seriously, but nothing you do can get Him to turn away from you in disgust. He always reacts by searching earnestly for new ways to come closer. He loves you too passionately, too fervently, to do less.

Do you think that if you swore at God, He would turn away? What if you told Him you hated Christianity, and the church and all its leaders, and vegetarian foods and tofu? What if you tied Him to a tree and pounded nails through His wrists and feet and laughed as you watched Him bleed? You would hear Him say, "I love you more than ever." The worse we act, the harder we try to push Him away, the more ardently He attempts to draw near.

Knowing that God is attracted to the deadest, smelliest places of our lives allows us to be totally honest with Him without the slightest fear of rejection. He comes incredibly near whenever He hears Christians utter anything like the following:

"Lord, You know that I want to murder that [insert swear word here] jerk!"

"Heavenly Father, I'm overcome with lust this morning. Right here in church I'm thinking about what it would be like to have sex with the woman giving special music."

"Jesus, I'd love to get high on heroine or get totally drunk right now."

"God, I'm furious at You for letting me become unemployed."

"Christ, I'm so discouraged. I don't care if I get to heaven or not."

We should never have to walk on eggshells with our Creator. Throughout Scripture the people who had the most mature relationship with God also had the most open, honest dialogue with Him. The rotten, deathlike places in their lives were fully aired, often with great passion.

Listen to David complain bitterly to God in the Psalms:

> And yet you have rejected, disowned and raged at [me]; you have repudiated the covenant with your servant and flung his crown dishonoured to the ground. . . . You have let his opponents get the upper hand, and made all his enemies happy. . . . You have aged him before his time and covered him in shame. Yahweh, how much longer will you hide? For ever? (Psalm 89:38-46, The Jerusalem Bible).

> Hear David cry out to God from the depths of depression and despair: "[I am] a man alone, down among the dead, among the slaughtered in their graves, among those you have forgotten. . . . You have plunged me to the bottom of the Pit, to its darkest, deepest place. . . . Wretched, slowly dying since my youth, I bore your terrors—now I am exhausted; ... you destroyed me with your terrors (Psalm 88:5-16, The Jerusalem Bible).

David praised God, but he also accused Him, blamed Him, and shook his fist at Him. Such deep emotions are characteristic of someone who knows God so intimately and trusts Him so fully that he can always tell Him exactly what is on his heart.

God knows everything about us anyway and longs to help. The apostle Paul wrote, "We have not a high priest who is unable to sympathize with our weaknesses" (Hebrews 4:15).

The wonderfully unique thing about Christ is that He not only has the sympathy and understanding of someone who comes to assist us like a firefighter or physician, He actually became one of the victims. He didn't simply observe our pain; He entered into it.

To illustrate, imagine burn victims who say to their doctor, "How can we have confidence in your treatments and prescriptions when you've never experienced deep and destructive wounds like ours? Why should we submit to your advice when you've never felt the searing pain that we've endured?"

The doctor is extremely concerned about his lack of credibility with his patients. One day he hears about a two-alarm blaze and rushes to the scene. When he arrives at the fire, flames are shooting out the upper-level windows of a three-story structure. Firefighters enter the building with high-pressure hoses and air masks.

The physician slips unnoticed into the building and makes his way up toward the heat and smoke. When he arrives at the top floor, he rushes past the firefighters and dashes directly into the flames. The horrified firefighters are at first stunned into inaction then spray water on him and manage to pull him out. The doctor sustains terrible third-degree burns over 70 percent of his body. He is a dreadful sight. He writhes and screams in pain on the way to the hospital.

He somehow survives and endures years of excruciating skin grafts and surgeries. His face and body are horribly, permanently scarred. As a result, no burn victim would ever again entertain the idea that he doesn't understand.

This imperfect analogy is an attempt to capture something of what Paul had in mind when he wrote, "For our sake he made him to be sin who knew no sin, so that in him we might become the righteousness of God" (2 Corinthians 5:21). The Savior voluntarily chose to be identified with sinners. The Gospel of Mark adds, "He was numbered with the transgressors" (Mark 15:28, KJV).

Christ understands well the debilitating effects of mental, emotional, and spiritual pain because that's what killed Him on the cross—not the nails. He died from inner torments that were heaped upon Him by others. Christ the sinless One walked directly into the fire of God's judgment on our sin and endured torments of mind and heart that we can only dimly imagine.

So what types of inner death did Christ experience?

One of Jesus' worst torments was the withering effects of *shame*. Paul tells us that the Son of God "was willing to die a shameful death on the cross" (Hebrews 12:2, TLB). Bible commentator F. F. Bruce writes, "To die by crucifixion was to plumb the lowest depths of disgrace."[5]

Today we have robbed the cross of its power to make onlookers puke, but in Christ's day it was "shame central." The cross now appears in church sanctuaries where sweet-smelling infants are dedicated, dreamy-eyed couples are married, and joyful hymns are sung. Calvary has been tamed, de-fanged, domesticated, sanitized, and house broken. But such shameful things were done to people on Golgotha that if an artist made a true-to-life rendering no one would want to hang it in their living room.

Christ also felt the crushing burden of our *guilt* as the sins of the entire world were credited to His account. "The Lord has laid on Him the iniquity of us all" (Isaiah 53:6, NKJV).

Jesus knows very well the terrible effects of *abandonment*. He experienced the horror of separation when He screamed out, "My God, My God, why have You forsaken Me?"

The Savior suffered the misery of *hopelessness*. The separation from His Father that He endured was so dark and deep that He lost hope in His own resurrection.[6]

He felt gut-wrenching *grief* at the thought that millions would reject His sacrifice.

Our Lord endured the trauma not just of physical *abuse* but mental and emotional abuse as well all during the trials and for the entire time He hung on the cross.

Christ knows very well all these sources of pain and more. And the very good news is that the Savior's resurrection Sunday morning was the victory over all the killing elements of Friday. When the Lord rose from the dead, He fully conquered everything that crushed Him on Golgotha.

As Morton Kelsey has observed, "The resurrection is the showing forth in the arena of this physical world that God wins, goodness wins, love conquers.... The forces of self-centeredness and evil condemned Jesus of Nazareth, judged him, crucified him. . . . They appeared to be victorious, but God raised Jesus from the dead. The risen Jesus demonstrated the victory of what He embodied—love, meaning, hope, joy, peace, transformation, never-ending growth."[7]

And Christ's victory is His pledge that He can minister effectively to the deathly hurts and troubles that harm our own hearts. As Paul put it, "Now he has made all of this plain to us by the coming of our Savior Jesus Christ, who broke the power of death and showed us the way of everlasting life" (2 Timothy 1:10, TLB).

Jesus can speak with enormous credibility about resurrecting the dead places within us because He Himself gained the victory over an inner death far worse than any human will ever have to endure. He has the impeccable credentials of someone who rose from a death caused by inward suffering so intense His heart literally burst. To borrow a phrase from Henri Nouwen, Christ is the "wounded healer."[8]

The deadly effects of shame, guilt, abandonment, hopelessness, unresolved grief, and abusive treatment that Christ experienced also plague Christians and non-Christians alike today. They lie at the root of enormous amounts of human pain and fuel myriad addictions and self-destructive behaviors. As Resurrector, Christ longs to come intimately close to each of these hurts and place our feet on the path to recovery and new life. As the psalmist has written, "The Lord is near to those who have a broken heart" (Psalm 34:18, NKJV).

All that can possibly stand in the way of inner healing is our unwillingness to come to Him and admit our need. Imagine someone in the advanced stages of leprosy placing fifty Band-Aid® strips on his body and saying, "I feel fine, really. I do have a slight tension headache, but otherwise I've never felt better!" Or imagine a person whose house is burning down telling the firefighters, "No need to get all excited. I think the old homestead looks quite stunning glowing so beautifully against the dawn."

It is just as absurd to deny the deadness that is within us all. The apostle Paul fingered our need when he wrote, "Even when we were dead . . . [Christ] made us alive" (Ephesians 2:5, Amplified). In order for healing to occur, people need to directly confront the smelly places of their lives. In a supportive, nonjudgmental atmosphere, they need to press beyond the natural desire to keep such places covered up and sealed.

One day Jesus received word that His close friend Lazarus had died. The Jews of that day believed the spirit of a dead person lingered about the tomb for three days, hoping that the deceased was not really dead. In such a case the spirit could re-enter the body. The belief also stipulated that on the fourth day the body would be in such bad condition that there was no possibility of resuscitation, and the spirit would depart.[9]

In light of that false understanding, Christ stayed away the requisite four days in order to be sure everyone was fully convinced that Lazarus had truly died. Jesus also stayed away because as Resurrector, He had so much life within Him that if He had been present, Lazarus could not have died.[10]

When Christ commanded, "Remove the stone from the tomb," Martha protested vehemently. "He stinks!" she said. "Don't let that putrid smell get out. Leave the stone in place. You've got to keep my brother's grave covered."

Jesus, in effect, replied, "Martha, you don't understand. What you so desperately want to avoid is actually a golden opportunity for hope and healing."

Like Martha, people today too often tell us in one way or another, "Don't remove that stone; keep the smelly parts of your life covered up. You shouldn't talk about such unpleasantness from the past." And so the pain festers and rots like a cancer.

Tragically no dead place is more frequently kept under wraps in many churches than mental and emotional illness. We talk openly about physical ailments and urge people to seek professional help. If someone has diabetes, they are encouraged to see the family physician and take insulin. When someone has a heart attack, people call the ambulance and have the victim whisked off to the hospital for possible surgery. We commend people with kidney disease for getting dialysis treatments.

But Christians all too often put illnesses and wounds of the mind and emotions in a different category. The idea is conveyed that the proper remedy lies primarily in strengthening one's personal relationship with God.

Jews in Jesus' day told people that their ailments were the result of a spiritual problem. People today can send the same kind of terrible message: "If you had a closer relationship with God, you wouldn't feel so depressed. If you trusted God more, you wouldn't have all those anxieties and fears. If you studied your Bible more thoroughly, you wouldn't have such terrible anger and insecurities." These sufferers not only have to deal with their mental and emotional pain; they also have to wrestle with the not-so-subtle, hurtful accusation that they are somehow spiritually defective.

It is not being weak to admit our inner need and seek help from a wide spectrum of resources, both human and divine. The most needy ones among us are those who refuse to acknowledge their own brokenness or think it is inappropriate to bring it into the light of day.

John Powell writes, "We must remember, if we want to love others truly, that these repressed and suppressed problems are very definitely impediments to love. They are our toothaches which keep us converged on ourselves, keep us from being ourselves, and keep us from forgetting ourselves."[11]

The dead places within us are not where God spends as little time as possible. Those are the places He loves to hang around the most. When we give Christ the master key to our lives, His divine fullness seeks out every area of need. Whether we perceive it or not, He works the hardest wherever we are having our greatest struggles. And as we respond to His creative workings, as another area of inner death yields to His life-giving power, He rejoices over us with singing. The journey may be long, with many ups and downs, victories and setbacks, but Christ will never pull away, never give up on His relentless, loving mission to make us whole.

---

[1] Dennis Smith, *Report From Engine Co. 82* (New York: Pocket Books, 1973), pp. 244–246.

[2] Ellen G. White, *The Desire of Ages,* p. 645.

[3] William Barclay, *The Gospel of John* (Philadelphia: The Westminster Press, 1975), 2:146.

[4] Carl F. Burke, *God Is For Real, Man* (New York: Association Press, 1966), p. 39.

[5] F. F. Bruce, *The Epistle to the Hebrews* (Grand Rapids, Mich.: Wm. B. Eerdmans Publishing Co., 1964), p. 352.

[6] Ellen G. White, *The Desire of Ages,* p. 753.

[7] Morton Kelsey, *The Drama of the Resurrection* (Hyde Park, N. Y.: New City Press, 1999), p. 92.

[8] Henri J. M. Nouwen, *The Wounded Healer* (Garden City, New York: Doubleday & Company, Inc., 1972).

[9] Leon Morris, *The Gospel According to John* (Grand Rapids, Mich.: Wm. B. Eerdmans Publishing Co., 1975), p. 546.

[10] Ellen G. White, *The Desire of Ages,* p. 528.

[11] John Powell, *Why Am I Afraid to Love?* (Niles, Ill.: Argus Communications, 1967), p. 72.

Chapter 12

Resurrection Life —Part A

In the spring of 1969, at age twenty-one, I awaited my turn to be baptized with mingled feelings of excitement and nervousness. The aqua-colored, fiberglass baptistry was built into the carpeted floor of the church altar. I had been assured that the water temperature would be above that of the open ocean.

The pastor in the tank finally motioned me forward. Six other candidates had already walked down the plastic runner, entered the water, and returned in the same direction with their full-length robes dripping. By the time it was my turn, the walkway had turned into a ten-foot-long water slide. Oblivious to such mundane concerns, I reveled in the lofty strains of "Just as I Am" sung by the expectant congregation.

I walked elegantly across the altar, placed my foot on the first step down into the baptistry, then slipped big time. It was not a pretty sight. Both legs went out from under me, and my arms flailed as I desperately tried to clutch at something stable. I wound up doing what many in the congregation later described as a creative variation on the classic cannonball. The pastor plucked me out of the water and yelled, "Wait for me!"

Such was my official entrance into the spiritual realm. Despite my inadvertent tumble, the occasion was certainly meaningful. Unfortunately, it was not nearly as meaningful as God intended it to be.

Baptism took on new importance for me when I came to realize that in Scripture it is intimately tied to the resurrection of Christ. In fact, unless we understand the deeper dimensions of baptism, we cannot appreciate the full significance of the empty tomb.

Many Christians think of the Resurrection only as something in the past that Jesus experienced or something in the future that believers will rejoice in at the Second Coming. God's plan, however, is that there be a third resurrection that happens in our hearts. Baptism is one of the major avenues through which that third resurrection can occur. It is a large part of God's answer to the question, "How does Jesus' resurrection impact my life today?"

Baptism is one of the main conduits through which we receive the same kind of life-giving power that brought Jesus forth from the tomb. It is God's intention that when we come up out of that watery grave, we enter what I call "resurrection life," a life of inner healing and wholeness in Him.

The first thing that occurs in baptism is that we experience death and burial. The apostle Paul writes, "We were buried therefore with him by baptism into death" (Romans 6:4). In the ancient world a person was not thought of as dead until they were buried.[1] So it is today that the fullness of our identification with the death of Christ is confirmed by being "buried" in the waters of baptism.

What needs to die is our spiritual self-dependence in which we run our own lives and rely on our own human resources. In Romans 6:6 Paul actually says that such self-dependence needs to be *crucified.* "We know that our old self was crucified with him." Christ invites each of us to join Him up on Golgotha's bloodstained cross. And then He asks us to be buried with Him in our hearts on a cold stone shelf in a garden tomb.

Of course the whole reason for being buried with Christ in baptism is that we can then be resurrected with Him. The apostle Paul wrote, "We were buried therefore with him by baptism into death, *so that* as Christ was raised from the dead by the glory of the Father, we too might walk in newness of life" (Romans 6:4, italics supplied).

As we come up out of the waters of baptism, the same Voice that spoke to Jesus in the tomb speaks to our hearts and says, "Come forth, thy Father calls thee." As He came out of the grave, we emerge from spiritual death to new life in Him.

If you have been buried with Christ, your resurrection to new life now is as certain as was the resurrection of the Son of God. Hear the assurance in the voice of Paul: "For if we have been united with him in a death like his, we *shall certainly* be united with him in a resurrection like his" (Romans 6:5, italics supplied). One Bible commentary explains the verse this way: "The apostle is not dealing here with our physical death and resurrection; he is dealing with our death to sin and our resurrection to Spiritual life." [2]

When NASA invites potential astronauts to enter the space program, they don't simply point them toward the heavens and wish them good luck. The space agency is committed to fully equipping these men and women to reach such lofty heights. They provide each astronaut with a $12-million space suit that supplies oxygen and offers protection against extreme temperatures, ultraviolet radiation, and micrometeoroids. [3] They also put the astronauts in a space shuttle whose two solid rocket boosters and three main engines provide 8.1 million pounds of thrust. More than forty individual thruster rockets give the shuttle maximum maneuverability. Approximately 31,000 custom-designed ceramic tiles enable it to withstand the 3,000-degree heat of re-entry. [4]

Likewise, the Trinity has taken great pains to equip us at the time of baptism with tremendous spiritual resources for our journey into resurrection life. New Testament scholar G. R. Beasley-Murray observes, "There is no gift or power available to man in consequence of the redemption of Christ that is not available to him in baptism." [5] Ruth Meyers identifies baptism as "the foundation for Christian life and ministry." [6]

Of course not all of God's gifts are received at the time of baptism. Salvation, for instance, occurs the moment we give our hearts to Christ. What God does at baptism is part of an infinite variety of ways He works in people's lives, but it is intended to be a very important part. It is designed to transform us in ways that no other experience can, and must not be reduced to mere symbolism. [7]

The spiritual resources that are provided at baptism enable resurrection life to permeate more and more of the dead places within us. They play a central role in God's ongoing process of renewal and restoration. This chapter and the next list several of those resources and briefly explore their meaning.

Uniting With Christ

In Romans 6:3 Paul starts right off with an amazing statement. He says that believers are baptized *into Christ,* which means they are in intimate union with Him. [8] Through baptism God establishes the closest relationship with us imaginable.

Paul underscores the connection of baptism and intimacy with God in Romans 6:5 when he says that through baptism Jesus and believers are "grown together" like two branches being grafted into one. [9] In Galatians 3:27 he also writes, "For as many of you as were baptized into Christ have *put on Christ"* (italics supplied). We become so enveloped in Jesus that it is like putting on a precious garment. On the Day of Pentecost the apostle Peter instructed his audience to be baptized *"in the name of"* Jesus Christ, which means to be in vital connection with Him.[10] (See Acts 2:38, KJV.)

Jesus Himself took the theme of intimacy through baptism to a wonderfully new level when He expanded it to include the entire Godhead: " 'Go therefore and make disciples of all nations, baptizing them in the name of the Father and of the Son and of the Holy Spirit' " (Matthew 28:19). Baptism, Jesus said, is the door to remarkable fellowship with the Trinity. Ever since the fall of Adam and Eve the Beings of the Godhead have been relentless in Their pursuit of intimacy with sinners. That has always been Their central, driving passion.

On His way to Gethsemane, the Son of God explained the level of closeness the members of the Godhead yearn to have with us when He uttered the extraordinary words, " 'As thou, Father, art in me, and I in thee, so also may they be in us' " (John 17:21, NEB). Jesus requests that we be as close to the Trinity as He and His Father are to each other!

Baptism could be seen as the marriage ceremony between God and us. As one Bible commentator put it, "Baptism represents the joining of the life of the believer in such close union with the life of Christ that the two become, as it were, one spiritual unity."[11]

Listen to the heavenly Lover reaching out to you: " 'I have loved you with an everlasting love; therefore with lovingkindness I have drawn you' " (Jeremiah 31:3, NKJV). And in the Song of Solomon, hear how affectionately He addresses you: "Behold, thou art fair, my beloved.... My beloved is mine, and I am his" (Song of Solomon 1:16; 2:16, KJV). In the Old Testament book of Zephaniah, God says that "he will exult with joy over you, he will renew you by his love; he will dance with shouts of joy for you as on a day of festival" (Zephaniah 3:17, The Jerusalem Bible).

God had you in mind when He said, " 'I will betroth you to Me forever; yes, I will betroth you to Me in righteousness and justice, in lovingkindness and mercy; I will betroth you to Me in faithfulness, and you shall know the Lord' " (Hosea 2:19, 20, NKJV).

I have seen a number of very happy couples up close as they recited their marriage vows. On average, brides are more relaxed at weddings than grooms. I'm usually rather nervous when I lead out because everything is done with such formality and an air of expectancy that I don't want to mess anything up. After the vows, there comes what used to be one of my favorite moments, when I say, "What God has joined together, let no man put asunder."

One time I sat in the congregation during a wedding and heard the officiating pastor say, "What *man* has joined together." My ears perked up. He'd obviously gotten his words twisted. There was a sweaty pause. I could almost hear the gears in his head whirring as the man hurriedly groped for a solution. He then made what I consider an outstanding recovery—"What man has joined together, *and God has ordained,* let not man put asunder."

At another wedding I heard a pastor say, "What man has joined asunder." It was hopeless. He just stopped, shrugged his shoulders, and started all over again. I now carefully read every single word of that hazardous sentence, just to be sure.

I can picture in my mind the moment at baptism when Christ looks at you lovingly and says "I do" and you reply. And then God the Father says with a confident, joyful voice, "What I have joined together, let no man put asunder." It is a marriage the Godhead will hold together tenaciously with every resource possible because They want it to be forever.

Knowing that God is eagerly pursuing each of us becomes an enormous source of self-worth, which is vital to resurrection life. Just imagine—the great, all-powerful God of the universe can't stand to live without us! He thinks about us day and night. He courts us for years, and His heart sings when we finally say "Yes."

Morton Kelsey writes, "God is love, and the experience of divine love meets our basic need to be loved. All of us have this same basic need, and unless we are loved, we cannot love others. Unloved people cannot will themselves to love. The heart of the experience of God is the inner knowing that I am loved; loved beyond my deserving, beyond my comprehension, beyond my earning."[12]

Cleansing From Guilt

After God knocked Saul (the apostle Paul) off his high horse on the way to Damascus, the once-proud Pharisee groped around on the ground, unable to see. He was put in touch with Ananias in order to receive back his sight. Afterward, Ananias told him, " ' "And now why do you wait? Rise and be baptized, *and wash away your sins*" ' " (Acts 22:16, italics supplied).

Can't you see Ananias and Saul wading out into a river or lake? The scourge of Christians everywhere was let down into the waters until they flowed up over his face and well-groomed beard. Ananias then strained to pull the burly man upright again. At that moment all the heinous sins Saul had committed, all the countless times he had rebelled against the Spirit, were completely forgiven and washed away.

The physical washing of baptism represents cleansing from guilt and the complete forgiveness of our sins, no matter how awful they may be. When we come up out of the water, we stand before God as if we had never sinned at all.

It doesn't matter whether we *feel* forgiven or not. Our assurance comes from what God has promised. One of the key elements of resurrection life is to apply the words of the apostle John to ourselves, "If we confess our sins, he is faithful and just, and will forgive our sins and cleanse us from all unrighteousness" (1 John 1:9, italics supplied).

Whenever we fall into sin again, we are to mentally re-live our baptismal experience of dying and rising with Christ and know by faith that we are forgiven.

Freedom From Guilt

On the Day of Pentecost, Peter told the gathered throng, " 'Repent, and be baptized every one of you in the name of Jesus Christ for the forgiveness of your sins; *and you shall receive the gift of the Holy Spirit*' " (Acts 2:37-39, italics supplied).

In the New Testament baptism was generally accompanied by a special impartation of the Spirit.[13] Beasley-Murray says that, "in the Acts and Epistles baptism is the supreme moment of the impartation of the Spirit and of the work of the Spirit in the believer."[14] Jesus Himself received an extremely significant infilling of the Spirit when He was baptized by John. (See Mark 1:10, 11; John 1:32, 33.) One Bible commentary observes, "[Christ's] experience reveals that water baptism and Spirit baptism belong together, that a baptism void of the reception of the Holy Spirit is incomplete."[15]

Many Christians pray to receive the special infilling of the Holy Spirit that the Bible calls the "former" and "latter" rain, utilizing an analogy from Middle Eastern seasons and agriculture. Perhaps these people need to be reminded that according to Scripture, they have already received a large portion of that blessing at baptism. They simply need to acknowledge by faith what they already possess.

John the Baptist declared of Jesus, " 'He will baptize you with the Holy Spirit and with fire' " (Matthew 3:11). Fire is a biblical symbol of purification.[16] (See Isaiah 4:4.) The Spirit is given to purify us from within, burning away whatever keeps us from experiencing the fullness of resurrection life.

God is anxious to not only deliver us from the guilt of sin but to permeate every aspect of our being with His abundant life. The Holy Spirit is eager to seek out all our hurting, broken places and make them whole. He can't wait to enter the dead, smelly, putrid places of our lives and resurrect them to His glory.

The ministry of the Spirit within our hearts is similar to the two times Jesus cleansed the Jewish temple of all the robbers, thieves, and assorted scoundrels.

The huge temple complex was made up of various "courts," or places of worship, built like concentric circles. The innermost area closest to the temple building was for the priests, followed by courts for the Israelite men and then the Israelite women. The outermost court was reserved for Gentiles, the non-Jews.

They could not go any nearer to the temple on penalty of death. This was the only place they could learn about the God of Israel and worship Him.

And it was in this Court of the Gentiles that all the Israelite barter was taking place. It was as noisy as the New York Stock Exchange. Jesus despised the irreverence and thievery. But the biggest problem was that the bedlam and chaos prevented the Gentiles from coming close to God.

So the Savior took matters into His own hands and overthrew the tables of the unscrupulous moneychangers, scattered the corrupt sellers of doves, and tossed them all out on their ear. He did what the Gentiles could not do for themselves. *He actively removed whatever got in the way of these non-Jews getting to know Him.* And through the Holy Spirit He is anxious to do the very same thing in the temple of our hearts today. Sadly, however, we often balk at His gracious efforts.

A friend of mine had to go in for surgery a while back to have something fixed inside of him. We have an excellent hospital in our area with expert surgeons. But suppose his trust level was so low that he tried to take matters into his own hands as he lay on the gurney in the surgical room.

He announces to the doctors and nurses, "First of all I want you to play this classical CD I brought. I don't want you people listening to any nerve-racking heavy metal rock music while you're tinkering around with my vital organs.

"I also want you to be sure and use this space-age scalpel I saw advertised on TV. Who knows how many times that old one on that tray over there has been used. I had this one sent overnight. It's high-grade steel with titanium edges and a special 'comfort grip, no slip' handle. And I want my friend Robert to record everything on video in case I have to sue."

They make the mistake of only giving him a local anesthetic, so all during surgery he's jabbering, "Did you wash your hands real good? Are you tying off *all* the arteries? I want to count all the instruments and sponges myself. What are you cutting now? You're not going anywhere near my liver, are you? How come you're sweating so much? I don't think this is going well. Look, close me up right now. I want a fourth opinion. Stop!"

We say that's absurd, but how many times do we do the very same thing as Christians and resist the Spirit's efforts? If we will just trust Him, the Spirit will, over time, employ a great variety of resources, both human and divine, to resurrect us in His image. He will lead us through a life-long process of inner healing that may at times appear dark and bewildering. It may involve many detours because of our willfulness and fears. But God will do whatever it takes to recreate us and make us whole.

In Romans 4 Paul gives us a stunning illustration of God's resurrecting, life-giving power. The Lord had promised Abraham that his children would be as abundant as the stars in the heavens. There was just one little problem. At the time God chose to fulfill that far-reaching promise Abraham was 100 years old and his wife, Sarah, was 89! They had stopped trying to blow out all the candles on their birthday cakes decades before.

But Paul tells us that upbeat Abraham "staggered not at the promise" (Romans 4:20, KJV). He staggered not for two reasons. He had faith that God could resurrect dead things. He also had faith that God is so powerful and so trustworthy that when He says He will do something, it is as good as done. As one translation puts it, "And this promise is from God himself, *who ... speaks of future events with as much certainty as though they were aleady past"* (Romans 4:17, TLB)!

As one Bible paraphrase puts it, "Abraham didn't focus on his own impotence and say, 'It's hopeless. This hundred-year-old body could never father a child.' Nor did he survey Sarah's decades of infertility and give up. He didn't tiptoe around God's promise ... and came up strong, ready for God, sure that God would make good on what he had said" (Romans 4:18, 19, *The Message*).

So one day God inspired white-haired Abraham to enter Sarah's tent with a conjugal sparkle in his eye that hadn't been there for ages. He also inspired wrinkled, hunched-over, varicose-veined Sarah to splash on some extra perfume and slip into a special toga.

Not long after their geriatric amoré, an embryo no bigger than a pinhead began to grow. Within four months Sarah started to show. After nine months, she was standing next to mothers in their early twenties, smiling gleefully and pointing through the nursery window at a bassinet with a blue nametag that read "Isaac."

Paul utilizes that miraculous story to point out that the Holy Spirit's ability to generate life does not depend on the material He has to work with. He has unlimited power to create and recreate. It is on that basis that we can have full confidence in His ability to fill all our dead places with resurrection life.

The apostle Paul wrote, "I pray that you will begin to understand how incredibly great [God's] power is to help those who believe him. It is that same mighty power that raised Christ from the dead and seated him in the place of honor at God's right hand in heaven, far, far above any other king or ruler" (Ephesians 1:19-21, TLB).

Reception of Spiritual Gifts

Although there are exceptions in Scripture, spiritual gifts usually accompany the special infilling of the Holy Spirit at baptism. University professor Gottfried Oosterwal defines a spiritual gift as " 'a special divine endowment, *given at the time of baptism,* to enable the believer to serve the church and to minister to those who have not yet accepted Jesus Christ.' "[17] These gifts are talents and abilities that are placed within us by God. The apostle Paul wrote, "Now God gives us many kinds of special abilities, but it is the same Holy Spirit who is the source of them all" (1 Corinthians 12:4, TLB). There are more than twenty different spiritual gifts listed in the New Testament, and every believer is guaranteed to have at least one.[18] (See 1 Corinthians 12; Romans 12; Ephesians 4.)

In order to experience the fullness of resurrection life, every Christian needs to know that his or her life has significance and purpose. One of the best ways to fill that need is to realize that God has equipped each of us at baptism for joyful partnership with Himself through the use of our spiritual gifts. It is an incredible partnership that will continue throughout eternity.

Discovering what spiritual gifts we were given at baptism and utilizing them to bless others can be a tremendous source of personal fulfillment. God is anxious to guide us into a ministry where we can feel effective. Each of us is vital to Heaven's plan. Not one gift can be left to languish. Not one person should be made to feel he or she isn't important.

Several days ago I rediscovered the program from my ordination into pastoral ministry on June 17, 1977. There is a black-and-white photo of me on the middle inside panel. Oh, the hair! It's all over my head and lapping down over my ears.

I was ordained at a large religious gathering in front of lots of people with a nationally known speaker presiding. Several officials were there from denominational headquarters. It was a big deal and I enjoyed it, but it would have been better if they hadn't done it that way. It could easily have made nonpastors in the pews think that my calling to ministry was somehow more spiritual or more important than theirs.

The truth is that the New Testament doesn't recognize different levels of calling. You may not be a pastor, but you are nonetheless a full-fledged minister for God.[19] Oosterwal again writes, *"By virtue of their baptism, in principle, all members participate alike . . . in the ministry, in the worship, in the mission, and in the charismata [gifts] of the church."*[20]

For Christians to enter more deeply into the newness of life that was theirs at baptism, they need to understand the very high status God has bestowed upon them. The Bible says that all believers are called to be "priests." The apostle Peter wrote to his church members, "You are the ones chosen by God, chosen for the high calling of *priestly work,* . . . God's instruments to do his work" (1 Peter 2:9, *The Message,* italics supplied). The great reformer Martin Luther wrote,

" 'Whoever has undergone baptism may boast that he is already a *consecrated priest.' "[21]

No believer should say, "I wish I could be involved in spiritual work full time like the pastor." As God's priest, you are a spiritually gifted minister, and your whole life is now a sacred endeavor.

---

[1] Ivan T. Blazen, *Baptism as Entry to the 'In Christ' Reality According to Romans 6 and Related Texts* (Unpublished paper, Loma Linda University n. d.), p. 19.

[2] John Murray, *The Epistle to the Romans* (Grand Rapids, Mich.: Eerdmans, 1975), pp. 218, 223; *The Seventh-day Adventist Bible Commentary,* 6:538, 539.

[3] Web site: http://www.sciam.com/2000/0600issue/0600working.html.

[4] Lou Drendel, *Walk Around Space Shuttle* (Carrollton, Tex.: Squadron/Signal publications, 1999), pp. 17, 25, 54, 27.

[5] G. R. Beasley-Murray, *Baptism in the New Testament* (Grand Rapids, Mich.: Eerdmans, 1994), p. 263.

[6] Ruth A. Meyers, Editor, *Baptism and Ministry* (New York: Church Hymnal Corporation, 1994), p. IX.

[7] Beasley-Murray, p. 263.

[8] Blazen, p. 12.

[9] *The Seventh-day Adventist Bible Commentary,* 6:538.

[10] Ibid., p. 147.

[11] Ibid., p. 537.

[12] Morton Kelsey, *Resurrection: Release From Oppression* (New York: Paulist Press, 1985), p. 184.

[13] Beasley-Murray, p. 275; *Seventh-day Adventists Believe ...* (Hagerstown, Md.: Review and Herald, 1988), p. 187.

[14] Beasley-Murray, p. 275.

[15] *Seventh-day Adventists Believe ... ,* pp. 186, 187.

[16] Leon Morris, *The Gospel According to Matthew,* p. 62.

[17] Gottfried Oosterwal, "Every Member a Minister? From Baptism to a Theological Base." *Ministry,* February 1980, 4–7, quoted in *Seventh-day Adventists Believe ... ,* p. 187, italics supplied; *The Seventh-day Adventist Bible Commentary,* 6:772.

[18] Oosterwal, pp. 4–7.

[19] Gottfried Oosterwal, *Mission: Possible* (Nashville: Southern Publishing Association, 1972), pp. 116, 117.

[20] Ibid., p. 110, italics in original.

[21] Ibid., p. 105, italics supplied.

Chapter 13

Resurrection Life
—Part B

I was more than a little excited because for the first time ever, my wife and I were going to visit the place where my aged grandmother grew up. Her family had lived in a remote area of Nova Scotia, in a tiny village that consisted of no more than a few widely scattered farm homes. For various reasons, by the early 1900s, all the villagers had moved away. Someone told me that all that remained of the houses was some rock-walled root cellars.

The only way to get there was by hiking five miles into the wilderness along a narrow, winding path. My wife and I had never attempted anything like that before. About 9:00 A.M. we headed out. I wore the typical hiking outfit for pastors—old suit pants, a long-sleeved shirt, and brand-new sneakers.

The sun shone bright as we strode confidently into the thick woods. Within fifteen minutes we encountered the first of a series of small mountains we would later call "life-sappers." Sweat poured off my brow. "I'm dying of thirst," I said, "give me some water."

My wife reminded me of my pre-trek words: "Forget water; it's way too heavy to lug around." We trudged onward.

By the time we reached the abandoned town, it was already afternoon. Exhausted and famished, I opened the plastic bag that held our lunch and peered down at two thin peanut-butter-and-jelly sandwiches. I ate my share slowly, then licked my fingers twice.

Nearby, an experienced hiker sat next to a miniature cook stove, heating tea. We intentionally walked his way. "Want something to drink?" he offered.

I forced a calm, "Sure, why not," then gulped several cupfuls.

We rambled around for two hours looking for Gramma's root cellar, any root cellar, but to no avail. I told my wife, "Without directions it's hopeless. We'd better head back now if we're going to beat the darkness." Foodless, water-less, we stumbled over hill and dale with increasingly shorter steps for four grueling hours and emerged from the forest just as the last rays of the setting sun dipped below the horizon.

Clearly, we were not equipped for the journey. It doesn't have to be that way, however, for our spiritual journey with God. In this chapter we will explore more of the resources He has provided through baptism to resurrect the dead places within us. These powerful resources are God's means of enabling us to enter into the fullness of resurrection life.

Becoming Part of the Body of Christ

The apostle Paul wrote, "By one Spirit we were all *baptized into one body*— Jews or Greeks, slaves or free—and all were made to drink of one Spirit" (1 Corinthians 12:13, italics supplied). The Scriptures portray the church as Christ's body, and we officially become part of it at baptism.

By calling the church His "body," Jesus makes it clear that the members are to be extraordinarily close-knit and interconnected. My heart, for instance, could not survive if it tried to function alone. If my stomach said, "I don't need all this togetherness stuff with those other organs," it would be dead in minutes.

Jesus further explained the degree of closeness He envisioned for His church when He prayed, " 'Holy Father, keep them in thy name, which thou hast given me, *that they may be one, even as we are one* ' " (John 17:11, italics supplied). Christ wants the church to become so united as a community that it resembles the unity within the Godhead itself!

For the church to function as a true biblical community, it must intentionally create an environment characterized by unconditional love and acceptance. Such a nurturing environment is absolutely essential if the resurrection life that new Christians receive at baptism is to be sustained and deepened. God wants people to be baptized into His body rather than to stand alone, in order to provide them with a caring community within which their new life can flourish and grow.

To ensure a successful launch by NASA, there are more than 500 experts at the headquarters in Florida who form the Primary Launch Team, the Engineer-ing Support Team, and the Mission Management Team. They religiously follow a 5,000-page flight preparation manual and do 25,000 pre-flight checks.[1]

The launch, however, is only the beginning of NASA's support. They know it would be disastrous if astronauts were left to make it on their own after liftoff. When the shuttle clears the tower, control of the mission is shifted to the Johnson Space Center in Houston, Texas.

The center consists of about 100 buildings and more than 15,000 employees. During the mission, experienced engineers and technicians monitor the astronauts and the shuttle twenty-four hours a day. Some of the key director groups include CAPCOM, which facilitates all communication, and FDO, which tracks maneuvers and trajectory. The Flight Surgeon monitors health parameters, and the Flight Activities Officer plans and supports all crew activities. Computer personnel also constantly compare what *is* happening to what *should be* happening and recommend adjustments.[2]

Continuous, comprehensive support is an absolute necessity for the success of the shuttle mission. That same kind of ongoing support is just as vital from the church community after a newly baptized person is launched into resurrection life. Pleading with the Body of Christ to fulfill its God-given role, Professor Laurence Stookey writes, "The church is . . . a community called into being at God's initiative. It is an essential assembly, without which those who come forth from [baptism] are still-born."[3]

For the church to be a biblically functioning community, it also needs to utilize and coordinate all the spiritual gifts it has been given. It is important for individual members to know their gifts. But it is also vitally important that all the gifts within the church function together in an effective way.

In the human body, the various cells and organs are wonderfully organized into various systems, such as the respiratory system, digestive system, circulatory system, nervous system, skeletal system, and so on. In a similar manner, the gifts of the Spirit need to be coordinated into a variety of life-giving ministries within the Body of Christ. Through such ministries the church breathes in the Holy Spirit, digests the Word of God, circulates life to every person, and stays in close communication with people's needs.

Tragically, in our eagerness to save souls, the spiritual gift of evangelism is often given top priority while the other restorative gifts are largely ignored. If the church is to minister effectively to the dead places in people's lives, it is vitally important that it organize such gifts as mercy, healing, encouragement, wisdom, knowledge, faith, discernment, intercession, and others.

Unless these gifts are being utilized well, how can the church be Christ's hands to release those held captive by addictions, enlighten those who are blinded by sin, and free those oppressed by years of brokenness and hurt? (See Luke

4:18.) Unless these gifts are effectively coordinated into restoring ministries, how can true wholeness come? Without them, how can the healing potential of resurrection life be fully realized?

In order for a church to highly value all of its spiritual gifts and utilize them well, it must discover the true measure of success as revealed in the following "Parable of the Hospital." The parable utilizes the familiar image of the local church as a hospital for sinners.

A three-story city hospital known as "The Church" was beginning to smell bad. An overpowering stench filled the hallways from numerous untended wounds and the many other neglected needs of the sick.

The six-person ambulance crew certainly could not be faulted. They faithfully responded to the urgent cries of those suffering from accident or illness throughout the troubled streets and filthy, rundown neighborhoods. Laboring in shifts, they regularly responded to 911 calls, picking up those in need and bringing them back to the hospital for help. Each person was gently placed in the lobby of the hospital before the crew sped away in answer to another call of distress. These hapless patients were then taken by orderlies to semi-private rooms and generally left to languish. Tragically, many ill and injured people died, most while waiting in their beds for assistance, several right in the lobby itself.

The problem was that few departments of the hospital were functioning well enough to provide much additional care. Two receptionists did a fine job of greeting each new arrival with a handshake and a smile. Five other staff members taught classes on a variety of health topics. The maintenance crew kept the building in mint condition, and the gift shop was lovingly managed by three senior citizens who sold handmade items on consignment. But many key services were missing entirely. No emergency room. No surgery department. No X-ray department. No cardiac care, pharmacy, physical therapy department, mental-health unit, cafeteria, laundry, or supply center.

There were certainly enough staff to fill the need, seventy-five in all, but most were untrained or simply chose not to get involved. Many of them did at least attend a weekly meeting to sing songs and review medical literature. All the patients were strongly encouraged to be present.

The Hospital Board was not unaware of the foul odor that permeated the facility. They felt, however, that their primary function was to keep that one ambulance running and rescue as many hurting people as possible. They defined success by how many new victims were brought into the hospital and rejoiced to see those numbers holding steady. Sure, there were problems, but at least these people were no longer on those awful, forbidding streets and were being given a chance at life.

One day a new CEO opened the first meeting of the board with a startling announcement. "I took the liberty of touring this facility recently and am deeply saddened by what I found. We say we care about hurting people throughout this large metropolitan area. But do we really?"

A long-time board member shot up his hand. "Of course we do. We have bent every energy to maintaining this building and keeping the ambulance running day and night. How dare you accuse us of not caring?"

The CEO replied calmly, "But, sir, what if we could have five ambulances, or ten, or even fifty? Couldn't we help far more people?"

Another board member answered in bewilderment, "But we only have the one crew that is willing and able, and they're out straight."

"I recognize that," the CEO responded patiently, "but what if we took those victims that the ambulance delivers every day and made them well. What if we built them up so they too could become ambulance drivers or carry on other vital work for this great facility?"

Another board member responded, "You've certainly got my attention. Please explain."

"You see," the CEO continued, "it really all begins with defining success in an entirely different way. Suppose we look not only at how many people are rescued, but also at what we do with them once they arrive. What if we start defining success by how well we are able to take hurting people and turn them into healthy, active participants in the mission of this hospital?

"To do that we must start bringing online all those missing services that are a vital part of making people whole. I have already shared this vision personally with some of our inactive staff. They confessed that the reason they opted out before is that they never felt effective driving ambulance. But I know we can use their skills in a variety of ways that will make them feel truly fulfilled."

The board voted to give the new emphasis a one-year trial.

Relatively soon two staff opened the emergency room part time, and the cafeteria produced at least one hot meal a day. Progress remained slow, with ups and downs, but five months later the X-ray department was functioning well. Next the surgery department operated several hours a week, and the pharmacy too. Eventually the smell in the hallways began to subside.

On a truly red-letter day, the hospital was finally able to purchase another ambulance. More important, they staffed it with a man who had come in months before with third-degree burns, a woman who had developed cancer of the lung, and a teenage victim of abuse. They were now strong and well trained to rescue others.

As the parable illustrates it is time for the church to abandon its nearly exclusive emphasis on winning converts and commit itself unreservedly to not only winning them but to healing and growing them in depth. Otherwise we will never reach as many sinners as God intended, and they will never experience the fullness of the resurrection life He has provided.

Prelude to an Incredible Reunion

The apostle Paul wrote, "If then you have been raised with Christ, seek the things that are above, where Christ is, seated at the right hand of God…. For you have died, and your life is hid with Christ in God. When Christ who is our life appears, then you also will appear with him in glory" (Colossians 3:1-4).

When Paul talks in these verses about dying and rising, he is referring primarily to the believer's commitment at baptism.[4] He goes on to say that the spiritual resurrection they experienced at that time was the prelude to their glorious physical resurrection at the second coming of Christ. Rising out of the waters of baptism points forward to that great reunion day when the righteous dead will all be raised to eternal life. Paul confidently declares, "If the Spirit of him that raised up Jesus from the dead dwell in you, he that raised up Christ from the dead shall also quicken your mortal bodies by his Spirit that dwelleth in you" (Romans 8:11, KJV).

This hope for the future is a crucial element of resurrection life. Laurence Stookey writes, "Through baptism, God tells us that history is headed somewhere…. God has a purpose, and pursues it relentlessly. In the end, that purpose will be accomplished. In this assurance we have hope and life."[5]

Hope sustains us when we feel like throwing in the towel. It keeps us going when the way seems terribly hard. It brightens our step during the routine of life. Hope shouts to us that death is not the end. As the psalmist has written, "Weeping may endure for a night, but joy cometh in the morning" (Psalm 30:5, KJV).

Years ago I was deeply moved as I read a book written by a pastor whose eight-year-old daughter, Laura Lue, contracted acute leukemia. Eighteen months after the initial diagnosis the family celebrated a memorable Christmas, but by the end of the day the little girl had begun to weaken. Two weeks later, on a Saturday evening, with snow falling gently outside her bedroom window, young Laura died.

Her anguished father wrote, "Here I am this morning—sad, broken-hearted, still bearing in my spirit the wounds of the darkness…. All I am doing is walking and not fainting, hanging in there, enduring with patience what I cannot change but have to bear."[6]

He clung desperately to the hope that eventually, on that great resurrection day, he and Laura Lue would "run again and not be weary," together they would "rise up with wings as eagles!" That day would surely come, but at the time of her death his pain was so deep that he could only walk and not faint. "That is enough," he continues, "O God, that is enough!"[7]

Suppose we were to fast-forward to the second coming of Christ. Imagine the scene when Laura and millions of other Christians are raised to eternal life. Thick darkness shrouds the earth. Ear-splitting thunder rumbles across the heavens like the booming of a thousand cannon. Lightning splits the sky with long jagged bolts of white-hot flame. The ground shakes violently from continuous earthquakes.

At a church cemetery somewhere in Massachusetts, stately trees crash on top of each other. A fierce hurricane-force wind sends branches flying. Suddenly the voice of the Son of God is clearly heard above the tumult, " 'Awake! Awake! Awake! ye that sleep in the dust, and arise' "![8] Granite grave markers shatter. The ground undulates like an angry sea and fractures wide open.

The redeemed emerge from their burial chambers. Guardian angels quickly come to be with the individuals they companioned for years. "Don't be fearful," they instruct. "You've been raised from the dead and will now live forever!" The redeemed ascend with their heads tilted back and their eyes focused upward toward the intense light overhead.

About a mile above the earth the angels eagerly begin to re-unite loved ones. Shouts and screams of recognition are everywhere.

"Dad, Dad, I'm over here!"

A woman is taken to her husband and two children. She yells, "We made it. Thank God we all made it!"

A mother is handed her baby who died from smallpox in the year 1908. She exclaimes, "Sarah, my little Sarah!" Sobbing with joy she holds the child tightly and kisses her repeatedly.

A son who died in combat on foreign soil during World War I is escorted to his mom.

A woman who died at the age of eighty-four in a nursing home sees her brother and calls out his name.

Shaking with joy and expectation, a daughter who was killed in her teens by a drunken driver is hurried to her parents and sister.

A wayward son who accepted Christ without telling anyone three weeks before he died in a motorcycle accident is taken to the rest of his family.

The sky overflows with gladness. The scene above that one graveyard is repeated countless times around the world. It is the wonderful day that the apostle

Paul pictured when he wrote, "The Lord himself will descend from heaven with a cry of command, with the archangel's call, and with the sound of the trumpet of God. And the dead in Christ will rise first; then we who are alive, who are left, shall be caught up together with them in the clouds to meet the Lord in the air; and so we shall always be with the Lord" (1 Thessalonians 4:16, 17). It is the great reunion morning, prefigured in baptism and made a reality by Jesus' cross and resurrection.

Our Inheritance

The apostle Paul wrote, "For as many of you as were baptized into Christ have put on Christ.... And if you are Christ's, then you are Abraham's offspring, *heirs* according to promise" (Galatians 3:27, 29, italics supplied). By virtue of our union with Christ that was publicly declared in baptism, we become heirs to an amazing future in the new earth.

Peter excitedly declares, "Blessed be the God and Father of our Lord Jesus Christ! By his great mercy we have been born anew to a living hope through the resurrection of Jesus Christ from the dead, *and to an inheritance* which is imperishable, undefiled, and unfading, kept in heaven for you" (1 Peter 1:3, 4, italics supplied). You can almost hear the apostle's heartbeat quicken as he contemplates what God has in store for His children.

One of the most amazing aspects of our future inheritance is the fact that we will reign as kings. Jesus promised, " ' "He who conquers, I will grant him to sit with me on my throne, as I myself conquered and sat down with my Father on his throne" ' " (Revelation 3:21).

After sin has been destroyed, Jesus' throne will be permanently transferred from heaven to this earth. This tiny planet will then become headquarters for the entire universe. (See Revelation 21:1-3.) Try to imagine how glorious the Lord's throne room will be—immense, magnificent, powerful, awe-inspiring. The floor appears translucent. The walls radiate multicolored rays. Various choirs periodically burst into spine-tingling songs of praise. First-time visitors stand in the entrance with their mouths wide open, too stunned to speak. Angels, unfallen beings from other worlds, and dignitaries of high office come and go constantly.

And there you are, way up on the throne itself, sitting next to Jesus with His arm around you. Most likely you also have your own seat of authority where you reign as overseer of some portion of the universe.

The Bible also says, " 'Therefore are they before the throne of God, and *serve him day and night within his temple' "* (Revelation 7:15, italics supplied). One commentary observes, "This promise would mean that the overcomer will hold a permanent, important place in the very presence of God."[9]

Once sin is eradicated, God will continue His amazing plans for the universe, plans that were temporarily interrupted by sin. And we will be at the center of it all as God's closest associates—studying, learning, planning, consulting, and supervising. We will be exalted in wide-eyed wonder to a place of mind-boggling privilege and responsibility.

The apostle Paul put it well. "In my opinion whatever we may have to go through now is less than nothing compared with the magnificent future God has in store for us" (Romans 8:18, Phillips). This little life is simply the internship for an extraordinary life to come.

Peter summarizes these thoughts by saying, "Praise be to the God and Father of our Lord Jesus Christ! In his great mercy he has given us new birth into a living hope through the resurrection of Jesus Christ from the dead, and into an inheritance that can never perish, spoil, or fade—kept in heaven for you" (1 Peter 1:3, 4, NIV). As you go about your routine each day, remember the incredible destiny that awaits you.

---

[1] Web site: http://science.ksc.nasa.gov/shuttle/countdown/launch-team.html.

[2] Web sites: www.jsc.nasa.gov/ and http://ftp.ksc.nasa.gov/shuttle/technology/sts-newsref/sts-jsc.html.

[3] Laurence Hull Stookey, *Baptism: Christ's Act in the Church* (Nashville: Abingdon, 1982), p. 29.

[4] *The Seventh-day Adventist Bible Commentary,* 7:210.

[5] *Baptism: Christ's Act in the Church,* p. 18.

[6] John Claypool, *Track of a Fellow Struggler* (Waco, Tex.: Word, 1974), pp. 14, 57, 58.

[7] Ibid.

[8] Ellen G. White, *Testimonies for the Church,* 1:60.

[9] *The Seventh-day Adventist Bible Commentary,* 7:759.

Chapter 14

Resurrection Life and Me

In this chapter I have chosen to write about times when I experienced some type of inner deadness, and the Holy Spirit ministered to me through *resurrection life*. It is motivated by my desire to put a human face on the themes covered in the previous three chapters. I wanted to do what I could to help move the theory from the head to the heart. The only example I felt competent to draw on was my own life. Although it would be much easier to share lesser difficulties, the subject of inner resurrection necessitates talking about more than surface issues.

My story is not extraordinary, but I fervently hope it will give you a measure of encouragement in the midst of hurts and hard times. I pray that it will also bolster your confidence that resurrection life is real and that it is very much available to you.

There is a danger in compressing time as I do here because it can lead to wrong impressions. I need to be clear that the darkness that characterized the episodes I focus on has not dominated my entire life. Most of the landscape of my fifty-three years has been fairly level, interspersed with a few mountaintop experiences and what felt like several pretty deep valleys. I am happily married to a very precious lady and have a marvelous twenty-three-year-old daughter. We laugh a lot and do things together a lot. We see the sun in our lives on many more days than the rain.

Death and Life in Pastoral Ministry

Deep down in my soul I am a devoted introvert. I relish curling up on the couch with a book. I covet the inner world of concepts and ideas. I am inwardly a very shy person. There were plenty of clues to my introversion early on when I was a teenager.

For instance, I had no dates during high school. No group dates, no double dates, no single dates, no dates of any kind. I was terrified of asking a girl out for a date. My best friend Charlie was terrified as well.

I remember one night in particular, however, when Charlie and I decided to go for broke and seek out some girls. I think I was in the eleventh grade. We drove around in his light-blue 1960 Ford dressed in our cruising uniforms— open paisley shirt, brown penny loafers, and tight bell-bottom jeans. We started patrolling expertly up and down Main Street filled with the thrill of the hunt.

We both spotted them about the same time—two high-school girls walking along the sidewalk, chatting and window shopping. I imagined Charlie and me walking arm in arm with those girls around town. These could be our future wives. These girls could be the mothers of our children!

Charlie and I looked at each other with that "Now or never" kind of look. It was a warm summer evening, and I had the window down on the passenger side. Charlie circled back and drove the car slowly along side them. They weren't more than eight feet away. He honked. I gulped hard, then blurted out, "Hey, you girls need a ride somewhere?"

They stopped, looked our way in disgust and replied, "Get lost, you creeps!"

I yelled at Charlie to hit it. He screeched tires, and we sped off into the night. About a mile down the road he pulled the car over, and we gave each other high fives. We had done it. We had actually talked to a couple of girls and lived to tell about it. That probably didn't qualify as an official date, but it was close enough for Charlie and me. It felt good to finally have a social life.

So, with that ultra-shy background, what career did I select? *Pastoring*— one of the most people-oriented, extroverted, up-front jobs on the planet.

I made that choice when I was half way through my engineering training at Northeastern University in Boston. All during my sophomore year I had felt intensely drawn to spiritual themes and entered into a lengthy period of careful Bible study on my own and with a local pastor. I became convinced that the second coming of Christ was very near and that the gospel had to be shared quickly with as many people as possible. I figured the best way to do that was to be a pastor. Within months, I left the university and transferred to a religious college as a theology major.

I knew almost nothing about pastoring. I received no guidance counseling. I had never even heard about spiritual gifts. Nonetheless, before I knew it, I had finished college, then seminary. By 1975 I was overseeing two churches in Massachusetts. After six years there, we moved north to pastor two churches in Maine. My melancholy personality kept me driving hard toward what I envisioned as success.

Overall, those were good years for our family. We met many wonderful people in the churches. I grew tremendously and learned invaluable lessons. I had the privilege of ministering to hurting people who confided their most agonizing struggles. I shared the joy of births and baptisms. I got to teach and preach great truths from the Word of God. I do not regret that period of my life at all. I had a vision of what church could be and pursued it with all my might.

The dissonance between my career choice and my true inner self periodically showed up in heightened anxiety, sharp mood swings, over-reactions to hurts, and lack of energy. I waved them off as part of the job description. I was far too busy saving the world to pay attention to any early warning signs of future trouble.

But what had begun as a quiet inner voice of warning eventually began demanding that I pay very close attention. The essential difference between who God created me to be and who I was trying to become ultimately caused a truckload of personal turmoil. The years of shoving inner pain down into the cellar of my life caught up with me.

I stayed in pastoral ministry as long as I could. Too long. Outwardly I appeared to be as successful as the next guy. But after many years of ministering to people on a regular basis, I became utterly drained. I was emotionally and mentally spent. My body rebelled big time. It began to ache and bleed and malfunction in all kinds of unnerving and creative ways. Sleeplessness, severe headaches, stomachaches, chest pain, and nausea were my companions for months. I vomited at home on a regular basis.

Physicians put me through every test ever devised by sadistic scientists. They thought I had kidney disease, then cancer, then heart disease. Finally a doctor simply sat me down and said, "Mr. Johnson, this is all because of stress. You've got to make some major changes in your life, now! Your health depends on it."

Not long after that discussion I started to seriously consider resigning. The devil scolded, "How can you even think about turning your back on your ordination?" My mind and heart struggled to know what to do.

By the end of 1983, I was so painfully ill that my wife and I both knew I had to resign. I reached toward the phone to call my conference president, then quickly pulled my hand back. A month later I touched the receiver without actually lifting it, then pulled back again. After several more weeks, I picked it up and dialed, then hung up in mid-ring. Then, with great trepidation and a big lump in my throat, I let the call go through. After telling my conference president, I notified the church members through a carefully worded letter.

Even though leaving pastoring eased my physical symptoms, the sense of personal failure that washed over me was difficult to bear. Thankfully, within a short period of time I felt drawn to study what the Bible has to say about the fact that we are all priests before God. I learned that He does not recognize higher and lower callings. He does not divide the believer's life up into sacred and secular.

As I read and prayed, resurrection life began seeping into my soul. The Holy Spirit taught me that I was not "leaving ministry." I was simply choosing to move from one area of priesthood to another. It was an enormous source of inspiration to know that I could hold my head high as God's minister in whatever profession I chose. The harsh sense of guilt and self-recrimination lifted.

An urgent, perplexing question remained. "What on earth could I do for work when all I'd trained to be was a pastor?" To my great relief the conference graciously offered to keep me on for a while doing local church audits.

After working all day at the conference office, I spent practically every night sending out resumes all across the country. I didn't get one reply. I took an aptitude test, scored high in accounting, and decided to enter night school to learn about debits and credits.

My job prospects continued to dim with each passing day. The future looked terribly bleak. I knew the conference couldn't keep me on indefinitely. Many nights I lay awake in bed worrying. I'd look over at my sleeping wife, then across the hallway into my six-year-old daughter's room, and tears would well up in my eyes. In my heart I cried out, "Oh God, what is going to become of us?"

My beloved wife was so incredibly supportive during this dark time. Her love and encouragement and her continued belief in me did not waver. My heart fills with gratefulness again as I write these words.

We often prayed such wrenching prayers as, "Send us some light, Father, some opening, anything." We leaned heavily on the words of Isaiah:

"Thus saith the Lord that created thee, O Jacob, and he that formed thee, O Israel, Fear not: for I have redeemed thee, I have called thee by thy name; thou art mine. When thou passest through the waters, I will be with thee; and through the rivers, they shall not overflow thee: when thou walkest through the fire, thou shalt not be burned; neither shall the flame kindle upon thee. For I am the Lord thy God, the Holy One of Israel" (Isaiah 43:1-3, KJV).

Friends we had known were wonderfully accepting and nurturing. The staff I began working with at the conference office regularly stopped by my desk to chat and offer encouragement. The Spirit graciously provided resurrection life through these crucial sources of support. My little spiritual community provided much-needed life and hope. I asked everyone to please pray earnestly. We claimed the promise, "I know the thoughts that I think toward you, says the Lord, thoughts of peace and not of evil, to give you a future and a hope" (Jeremiah 29:11, NKJV).

In my heart of hearts I felt convicted that a job in conference treasury work would be ideal. The only possibility of me getting such a job was in my own conference, but I had very little training and there was absolutely no opening. One assistant treasurer had only been there for a short time and enjoyed it thoroughly. The other, Donny, had frequently testified, "I love this part of the country and can't imagine ever moving away."

Then, almost two months later, I overhead Donny tell someone, "You know, I've got some close friends in California who are itching to get me out there. I really don't know what's gotten into me, but I've decided to go. I'm really excited about it."

My ears perked up, and my heart began to pound. *Oh Lord,* I thought, *is it possible?* I phoned my wife and asked her to start praying right away. After Donny announced his departure, I wished him well and immediately applied for his job. I was a long shot at best.

An unusual, heaven-sent feeling of peace and calm came over me. I sensed the Spirit taking charge of circumstances. I dared to imagine that the darkness could be turned into a day of new opportunities and joy.

The conference executive committee met three weeks later. I waited nervously by the phone. About 5:00 P.M. the treasurer called and said, "Welcome to the treasury department, Kim. You're the new assistant!"

I said, "Thank you so very much," hung up the phone, and screamed.

The treasurer later told me that the timing of my resignation from pastoral work was the key. "It filled a genuine need we had and gave us an opportunity to observe your work firsthand. We saw how meticulous you were with church audits. And you had time to learn the basics from your accounting classes. And of course the perfect timing of Donny's decision to leave. The Lord certainly had His hand in this one."

I gladly took all the other accounting courses the local business college offered and have been in conference treasury work now for almost twenty years.

The Holy Spirit let me hit rock bottom so I would ask for help, then stepped in and lovingly guided me toward His solution. There had been inner deadness, but there was now also life.

Accounting fits well with my preference for working with things rather than people. It suits my melancholy need for structure and order because numbers add up today the same way they did yesterday. When I pastored, it was hard to point to something tangible at the end of the day that I had completed, which I found difficult. But in accounting, clearly defined tasks get finished, and they stay finished. I also find an office environment very uplifting as opposed to the lone-ranger setting for pastors. The Holy Spirit planned all of this way ahead of time. He worked patiently and placed me in a career and work environment where I could experience deeper dimensions of resurrection life. The following fourteen years were generally happy ones for my family and myself.

Death and Life in Knowing Myself

Sometime in the spring of 1997 I had two job offers in the Seventh-day Adventist denomination that entailed much greater responsibility. They were both located farther south and came in the dead of winter when many Mainers have the "Why on earth don't I live in a warmer place?" blues. People urged that these were once-in-a-lifetime opportunities. Each one provided a significant new challenge and a position further up the organizational ladder.

I had rejected other offers of employment in the past without much anxiety. But this particular decision nearly paralyzed me. I wrestled with the inner deadness of fear and doubt that swept over me. After struggling with the options for several days, I felt utterly drained. Languishing in perplexity, I visited my Christian counselor and pleaded tearfully, "What choice should I make? What should I do?"

He wisely began probing underneath the immediate pain to discover what was fueling it. He asked if I had strong feelings of frustration in my life. At one point he inquired, "Is there some part of who you are that you're ignoring, that needs fuller expression?"

Something resonated strongly within me. The answer came with a clarity and force that was startling. I paused, then looked up and told him, "I believe that a big part of me is a creative, visionary person, with a passion to write for God." I had never articulated that thought to anyone before, and never that clearly, that boldly, even to myself.

Immediately the presumption and audacity of what I had said soured into a sharp inner rebuke. My mind scolded, "You a writer? Give me a break! You pompous fool!"

It was true that there was hardly any outward evidence to support my newly voiced dream. I had nothing of consequence published.

I forced out the words, "I don't want some big, fancy job. I don't care two figs about climbing an organizational ladder or having more authority. I just long to be able to sit up in my little room at night and . . . and write."

The counselor replied, "Then you need to believe in what you are saying and go for it. I'll be here to help." At that moment I discovered the right side of my brain, the side that houses the Arts Department.

I sat there in silence. A very heavy load had just been lifted. Resurrection life entered as my heart reached toward the future my words had depicted. Within minutes an unexpected boldness seized me, and I decided to go for it. I would heed that passionate inner voice calling me to write, no matter how insecure I felt about it at the time. I would give it my best shot and leave the results with God.

My counselor and I soon realized that I had been subconsciously rebelling against the two job offers because something inside of me sensed that they would cause so much stress and eat up so much time that I would have little opportunity to write. I immediately turned down both job offers.

One of the first articles I wrote for a denominational magazine was about the "empty nest syndrome" my wife and I experienced when our only child left home for boarding school. I was surprised at the strong emotion I felt as I wrote.

My heart pounded as I sent the article away. After several weeks a letter arrived from the magazine with my name on it. I whispered a silent prayer as I opened it. "Mr. Johnson," it said, "we are pleased to let you know that your article has been accepted for publication." I shouted to my wife. We hugged. That night we went out to eat to celebrate.

After having several articles published, I felt drawn to take a giant step. I contemplated writing a book about a topic that had been close to my heart since college, the sufferings of Christ. I had actually submitted a manuscript on that theme in 1982, but it was rejected. When I got that rejection slip, after expending so much effort, something inside me shriveled up. I didn't write again for fifteen years, which effectively shut down most of my creative side for that entire period.

I now wondered if I really wanted to risk that same kind of hurt. What if my book was rejected again? How would I react? Would it discourage me terribly? The Holy Spirit tapped me on the shoulder and reminded me of my commitment to write for the Lord and leave the results with Him. I decided to devote the next twenty-four months to the project. I did extensive additional research and spent countless nights writing and revising the old material. I titled the book *The Gift*.

At last I stood at the post office clutching the bulky package with my precious manuscript inside. The earlier rejection flashed through my mind. I paused, drew in a deep breath, then I dropped the package into the mailbox. Waiting was difficult.

Two months later I was at the Adventist Book Center during camp meeting and was introduced to Rhea Harvey from Pacific Press. When I told him my name, he smiled and said, "Oh, yes, our committee just reviewed your manuscript, and it was accepted." How my heart sang! Another huge piece of my life fell into place. I knew then for sure that the Holy Spirit had taken me much further into resurrection life.

Since the publication of that book I have received emails from readers as far away as New Zealand. Each response has been both humbling and deeply rewarding. It is a remarkable feeling to know that God is using the words that my fingers typed to touch thousands of lives.

I have in many ways now come full circle. My seminary training and pastoral years have been an invaluable help in writing about theological topics and church life. As I wrote this book on the Resurrection, I again felt so privileged to be able to minister for God through the written word.

Death and Life in Facing Depression

Piece by piece the Holy Spirit was peeling back one layer of my life at a time, as I would allow, and leading me toward wholeness. The next layer, however, was one of the most painful ones. I don't even remember the circumstance at the time, but in January 1999 I began to slip into the deepest depression I have ever experienced. People who say, "Hey, buck up, everyone has the blues from time to time," have no clue how awful the darkness can become. It was hard to tell why, but I was steadily sinking into a crushing sense of hopelessness and despair and felt powerless to stop it.

One morning I just sat on the living-room couch, held my head in my hands, and sobbed. I somehow got myself going and went to work, but then sat at my desk feeling overwhelmed. Tears flowed again. My wife, who works in the neighboring office, came in, looked at me, and started crying herself. We decided to go home.

Frightened, I phoned my former counselor who had now retired. He made an immediate referral to another Christian counselor downtown, and my wife and I went to see him that afternoon. All I can tell you is that God sent that man into my life. My eyes mist over even now as I think about it. The counselor reassured me that healing could come. We set up several more appointments.

He then said something I never thought I would ever hear. "I want you to go right now and see the staff psychiatrist to be evaluated." Seeing a counselor was one thing, but a psychiatrist!

I entered his office downcast and extremely nervous. My self-esteem was hovering around minus fifty. After a series of questions he told me, "I'm going to put you on some anti-depressant medication." I slumped down in my chair and felt defective, weak, and ashamed. *I can't even make it without medication,* I thought. That evening I reluctantly took my first pill.

Two nights later I told the small group my wife and I attended, "We have just gone through what has got be one of the worst days of our lives." They ministered to us through their spiritual gifts and laid hands on me, offering wonderful prayers for healing and strength.

During the next several weeks I could feel a marked improvement. I continued to take the medication and go for counseling. Soon the depression lifted.

I have learned that the lack of neurotransmitters that carry signals between nerve cells in the brain can often be a major cause of depression. Medication helps correct that chemical deficiency. So why then should someone like me on anti-depressants be viewed any differently than a diabetic on insulin or a person who takes medication for high blood pressure?

Having experienced so much needless pain over the years because of my refusal to seek professional help, I am angry that society stigmatizes people like me who face mental or emotional problems. Too many churches aren't much better. I have a new appreciation for the courage it takes for people to press through such terrible distortions and seek help.

Working with my current counselor, I have made very significant progress. I am growing in ways that, frankly, surprise me. We examine the past but focus mainly on the present. People react differently to circumstances, but some of the early factors that damaged me inwardly were an alcoholic father and a conflicted and divided home. We also began probing the long-buried inner wounds I suffered during childhood from being the object of a town bully's intense ridicule for several years.

The Spirit is healing hidden hurt and leading me once again into a deeper experience of resurrection life. He has accomplished the words of Isaiah, "He gives power to the weak, and to those who have no might He increases strength" (Isaiah 40:29, NKJV).

Besides professional assistance, God continues to minister to me through the life-giving kindness and understanding of my spouse and daughter. Close friends and small groups have been another important means of ongoing support. My life is much more balanced now. I enjoy working with the left side of my brain all day at accounting, and at night my right brain is raring to get started writing.

God is not finished with me yet because He is relentless in His pursuit of my wholeness and joy. But I am deeply thankful to the Lord for already fulfilling so faithfully the promise recorded by the apostle Peter:

> His divine power has granted to us all things that pertain to life and godliness, through the knowledge of him who called us to his own glory and excellence, by which he has granted to us his precious and very great promises, that through these you may escape from the corruption that is in the world because of passion, and become partakers of the divine nature (2 Peter 1:3, 4).

As we look back on the resurrection of Christ and His appearances to the first-century believers, our hearts can be filled with wonder at the life and love that flowed from the Son of God. His emergence from the tomb made all things new. God's re-creative, death-defying power burst forth from the garden grave with such brilliance and intensity that it shines down to our own day in undiminished glory. The raising of our Lord lit a flame that has grown into a global conflagration of grace. The worst of sinners can bask in its restorative influence and be made whole. The Resurrection is the guarantee of final victory, not only throughout the cosmos, but also within our own struggling, sin-damaged hearts. It is God's pledge that His love will surely prevail and that our ultimate inheritance will be nothing less than unending, Christ-centered joy.

> I turned to see whose voice it was that spoke to me; and when I turned I saw seven standing lamps of gold, and among the lamps one like a son of man, robed down to his feet, with a golden girdle round his breast. The hair of his head was white as snow-white wool, and his eyes flamed like fire; his feet gleamed like burnished brass refined in a furnace, and his voice was like the sound of rushing waters . . . When I saw him, I fell at his feet as though dead. But he laid his right hand upon me and said, "Do not be afraid. I am the first and the last, and I am the living one; for I was dead and now I am alive for evermore" (Revelation 1:12-18, NEB).

Discussion Questions

Chapter 1: Love's Last Breath

1. How do you react when you see someone treated unjustly as Christ was? What kinds of ill treatment of others anger you the most?

2. Tell about a time when you had a hard time breathing.

3. What is your reaction as you read about Jesus' battle to breathe? Why? (Circle one.)
   a. Fear
   b. Anger
   c. Admiration
   d. Suspense
   e. Hope
   f. Other

4. Would it ever seem appropriate to rejoice at someone's death as Heaven did at the death of Jesus?

5. How do you feel about being around a cemetery, especially at night?

6. What do you think Jewish Christians told their children on Friday night regarding the death of Jesus earlier that day?

7. Has there ever been a time when something you strongly hoped for turned to ashes? Describe your feelings.

Chapter 2: Peter's Grief

1. Tell about a time when your good intentions got you into trouble.

2. What is your initial reaction after failing personally? Explain. (Circle one.)
   a. I get down on myself
   b. I blame others
   c. I eat a lot
   d. I try to learn from my mistakes
   e. I want to be alone
   f. Other

3. Tell about someone who believed in you and how it affected your life.

4. Peter phones you and tearfully tells you all about his denials. What do you say?

5. When it comes to being "adventuresome," like Peter walking on the waves, how would you describe yourself? How much risk can you tolerate?

6. If you were one of the twelve disciples, what would you have said to Peter after he walked on water and sank?

7. If you had been there at the cross when Jesus died, what are the chances you would be thinking about a resurrection? Why?

Chapter 3: Mary Magdalene's Loss

1. In your view, what is it about incest that makes it particularly destructive to the victim?

2. How would you feel if a notorious prostitute visited your church and sat in your pew?

3. Have you ever had to move to a new place where you didn't know any-one? What insight does that give you into how Mary might have felt in Magdala?

4. What kept Mary from committing suicide in Magdala before she met Jesus?

5. Which of the following characteristics of Jesus was most responsible for the intensity of Mary's love? Explain. (Circle one.)
   a. Teachings
   b. Trustworthiness
   c. Patience

d. Acceptance
e. Healing power
f. Other

6. If you were kneeling next to Mary at the sealed tomb on Friday, what would you say or do to console her?

7. What helps you to trust other people? How does that relate to trusting God?

8. What hurts or disappointments from your past get in the way of relating well to God today?

9. Has there been a time when you knew that God specifically delivered you from some type of trouble? How?

Chapter 4: The Greatest Miracle

1. If Satan instructed his evil angels regarding how to keep you sealed up in the darkness of discouragement, what would he say?

2. Tell about a time when you were afraid of the dark. How did you deal with it?

3. You are a devout Jew on your way to the temple on the Friday evening of Jesus' death. What are you talking about with your companions?

4. What kinds of supernatural weapons can you imagine Satan and his evil angels had?

5. Describe a time when you were filled with eager anticipation of some upcoming event.

6. You are peering out from behind a big cypress tree when Jesus emerges from the grave. What do you see, hear, and feel?

7. Why didn't the Savior remove His own grave wrappings?

8. To try and grasp God the Father's emotion when He saw Christ after the Resurrection, describe the greatest celebration or reunion you have ever experienced.

Chapter 5: The Women First

1. Tell about a time when you were bursting with good news.

2. Have you ever lost something of great value? How might that be like Mary Magdalene's hurt at seeing that the body of Christ was missing?

3. What does the fact that the Resurrection story gives such prominence to women tell you about how God relates to downtrodden people? How could that help when you feel put down or cast aside?

4. Describe a time when something seemed "too good to be true." How did it turn out?

5. What is the first thing the resurrected Christ will say to you when you meet?

Chapter 6: Remarkable Restorations

1. Describe your reaction if you had been at Len's funeral when he woke from the dead. What makes the resurrection of someone so much more startling and impressive than any other miracle?

2. Why did Pilate believe in Jesus' resurrection but the disciples didn't?

3. If you lived in Judea and didn't want to believe in Christ's resurrection, how would you explain away the appearance of these giants from the past?

4. Why did God choose to resurrect only martyrs?

5. You came up out of the grave at the same time as Jesus and are now headed into Jerusalem. Where do you go, and what is going through your mind?

6. What does the phrase, "God never sees crowds, only individuals," mean to you?

7. If someone you know acts in as untrustworthy a manner as Peter did, how can he or she regain your trust? What part could you play in making that happen?

8. What gave Peter credibility as a leader after the Resurrection even though he had made such big mistakes?

Chapter 7: Two Eye-opening Meals

1. Why did Jesus never tell the Emmaus disciples who He was?

2. What would help you to have confidence that Christ is walking by your side during times of perplexity and confusion?

3. If Jesus showed up unexpectedly for dinner at your house, what exactly would you serve?

4. What makes sharing a meal one of the best ways to get to know people?

5. You are in the upper room prior to seeing Jesus. What would convince you to open the door to someone on the outside?

6. Who would be the most startling person to show up at your house today? Why?

7. Describe a time when God surprised you by showing up with a blessing in the midst of a period of sorrow or anxiety.

8. What would it take for you to believe reports that a dead person had come back to life?

Chapter 8: Beyond Reasonable Doubt

1. Can a Christian have strong doubts and strong faith at the same time?

2. Why has Thomas become so identified with doubting?

3. If Thomas were preaching in your church, what could he say to counteract the impression of him as a doubter?

4. Do you agree that Thomas probably had a "melancholic" personality? Why?

5. How does the fact that Christ sometimes intentionally stayed away from people affect your "God-concept"?

6. How do you hang on to God when He seems to be a million miles away?

7. Has God allowed you to walk through some wilderness territory lately? How did it affect your relationship to Him?

8. What word best captures the way you would describe Thomas after reading this chapter? Explain. (Circle one.)
   a. Trusting
   b. Courageous
   c. Doubting
   d. Loyal
   e. Insightful
   f. Other

Chapter 9: My Brother's Keeper

1. Which of your siblings were you closest to? Why?

2. Describe a humorous memory you have of you and your siblings.

3. If you heard the boy Jesus crying in His bed at night, what would you say or do to comfort Him?

4. Why does rejection hurt so much? What ways are there to deal with it?

5. Why is it so important that a person's family believe in him or her? What can happen if they don't?

6. Are there areas of your Christian experience in which you have a hard time seeing and hearing spiritually? How do you know when that is happening?

7. Why do you think that Jesus' brothers believed the testimony of James but not the words of Christ Himself?

Chapter 10: Group Flight to Glory

1. All of sudden you start rising up from the ground. Describe what you are thinking and feeling.

2. What parts of you feel imprisoned and would like to break out? What would it take for that to happen?

3. Imagine a typical day in the life of Moses, Enoch, and Elijah in heaven before the birth of Christ. What are they doing?

4. What event here on earth could help you envision the reaction in heaven at the moment when Christ and the redeemed arrive there?

5. How could the disciples possibly still hang on to the idea of setting up an earthly kingdom after witnessing the death and resurrection of Christ? What had they not learned from those momentous events?

6. Have people ever clapped for you? When? How would it feel for millions to do that in heaven?

Chapter 11: God of the Dead Places

1. Based on this lesson, how would you define what is meant by a "dead place" in a person's life?

2. People don't usually draw closer to us when we act or smell bad. How does that human reaction affect our picture of God? How can that change?

3. Which of the following dead places have you seen most often in people's lives? How do they usually deal with it? How could this lesson help?
   a. Anxiety
   b. Depression
   c. Loneliness
   d. Insecurity
   e. Hopelessness
   f. Shame

4. How would you interpret the statement, "In a church where everyone appears strong, no one grows"?

5. Why does society so often place a stigma on mental and emotional illness? How can that be altered within your church?

6. What gets in the way of your fully believing and trusting that God will never reject you?

7. What part of your life is most in need of the resurrecting power of Christ?

Chapter 12: Resurrection Life—Part A

1. What would you give as a definition for "resurrection life"?

2. If you have been baptized by immersion, how meaningful was it for you at the time?

3. If you have not been baptized by immersion, would you consider such an experience?

4. Even if you believe in your mind that God is intensely in love with you, how fully do you believe that in your heart? What is the difference?

5. Would you feel comfortable saying that right now, by the grace of God, you are completely forgiven and saved? Why or why not?

6. What does it mean that we are given a "special infilling of the Holy Spirit"? What difference can that make in your everyday life?

7. What do you believe are your "Spiritual Gifts"? What gifts do the group members see in each other?

Chapter 13: Resurrection Life—Part B

1. What have been the most significant aspects of your personal journey into "resurrection life"?

2. Do you feel accepted and valued in your local church as a member of the body of Christ?

3. Do you know what part of the body of Christ you are? How could you find out?

4. What spiritual gifts would be the most helpful for each of the following needs? How?
   a. Grief
   b. Depression
   c. Low self-worth
   d. Life decisions
   e. Burnout

5. In what area of your life do you most need support right now from fellow Christians?

6. What is the main lesson you learned from the parable of the hospital? How could you help your church implement that lesson?

7. Who will you be looking for on the resurrection day? What is the first thing you will say to them?

8. When you sit down next to Jesus on His throne, what will He whisper in your ear?

Chapter 14: Resurrection Life and Me

1. What parts of Kim Johnson's personal journey into resurrection life could you identify with the most? Why?

2. Do you feel well matched to your vocation? If not, what can help?

3. What are the strengths and challenges of being an introvert? Is it easier to be an extrovert?

4. How would you react to someone who said, "I don't need any help from others to deal with my troubles. I get along just fine, thank you"?

5. Are you at a turning point in your life right now? How can the group help?

6. In what do you feel passionately about investing your time? What resources do you need for that to happen?

Now that you've been touched by *The Morning*,
Don't neglect *The Gift.*

Kim Johnson first burst on the publishing scene with *The Gift*—a breathtaking look at Christ's sacrifice on the cross.

"The best news on the planet is that the cross changes lives, permanently," says Johnson. "It reaches down into the most discouraged, fearful, selfish hearts and brings renewal."

The writing is gritty, vivid, and real. Through Johnson's inspired prose the reader witnesses Christ's majesty and splendor before the creation of Earth, and feels the unspeakable horror of rejection and torture as the Creator pays the ultimate price for salvation on Calvary. *The Gift* is a reading experience that will leave its mark on your heart forever. It is available at Adventist Book Centers and online at www.AdventistBookCenter.com.

0-8163-1768-2. Paperback. US$11.99, Cdn$18.99.

What people are saying about *The Gift:*

Halfway through reading the Introduction I had to pause, close the book, and swallow a large lump in my throat before I could continue reading. Kim Johnson's writing gripped both my mind *and* my heart as he walked me through the many facets of Jesus' sacrifice. I treasure this book because it widens my thinking and deepens my appreciation for the greatest Gift ever given.
—Shelley Schurch

Kim, you have made me fall in love with Jesus all over again. And I never want to fall out of love with Him and for Him. I have such a feeling of gratefulness that only can be explained by the words in your book! Thank you, thank you, for making Him so real and personal.
—Marlene Smith

Thank you! Thank you! Thank you! for writing on this subject. The Cross is the KEY to everything. And the highest spiritual experience we can have is to identify with Jesus Christ in the "fellowship of His sufferings."
—Ervin Thomsen, Pastor

Order from your ABC by calling **1-800-765-6955**, or get online and shop our virtual store at www.adventistbookcenter.com.

The author would enjoy receiving your reactions and comments. Contact him by email at: KAllanJohnson@compuserve.com.